Contents

The seal of the Llantrissant and Taff Vale Junction Railway Company.
Welsh Industrial and Maritime Museum

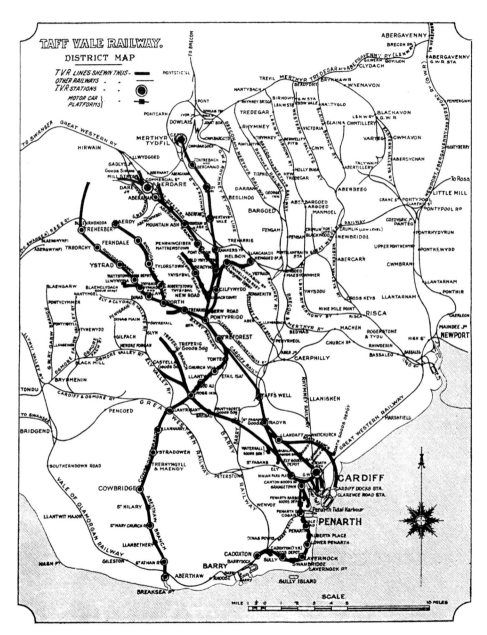

Taff Vale Railway map, 1922.

The
Llantrisant Branches
of the
Taff Vale Railway

A History of the
Llantrissant and Taff Vale
Junction Railway

and the
Treferig Valley Railway

by
Colin Chapman

THE OAKWOOD PRESS

British Library Cataloguing in Publication Data
A Record for this book is available from the British Library
ISBN 0 85361 481 4

Typeset by Oakwood Graphics.

Printed by Henry Ling Limited, The Dorset Press, Dorchester.

Llantrisant station in the early years of this century, looking along the South Wales main line towards Bridgend. Trains from Pontypridd crossed the main line to reach the Cowbridge bay on the extreme left of the picture. *I. Pope Collection*

Published by
The Oakwood Press
P.O. Box 122, Headington, Oxford

Preface

For many people the Taff Vale Railway (TVR) conjures up images of a four track main line crammed with the produce of busy mining valleys. There was, however, another side to the railway, represented by a number of straggling single track branch lines, with relatively limited traffic. For a large part of the 19th century, the company, under the inspiration of its forceful chief officer, George Fisher, pursued a speculative policy of developing or encouraging new lines in advance of traffic. In the case of the Rhondda branches and certain other lines, this policy proved spectacularly successful, but in others it was somewhat less so, leaving a legacy of little-used branch lines.

Another feature of the growth of the TVR was the way in which the company made use, directly or indirectly, of nominally independent satellites in pursuit of its strategic aims. By the time this disparate empire was consolidated in 1889, there were no less than nine such concerns leased and worked by the TVR.

The Llantrisant branches, formed by the Llantrissant and Taff Vale Junction Railway (L&TVJR) and the Treferig Valley Railway, came into being through such nominally independent companies. The original L&TVJR main line (later known as the Llantrisant branch) always carried a worthwhile traffic, although it was relatively modest compared with other parts of the TVR. However, the later extensions of the L&TVJR (the Common branch and Llantrisant No. 1 Railway) and the Treferig Valley Railway were very much in the speculative tradition. The former lines were relics of a little-known campaign in the Gauge War in South Wales, while the latter failed to encourage the development of the mineral resources of the district which it served.

The network formed by these lines had a complex history and a character of its own and as such merits closer attention in the form of an independent study.

A comment on the spelling of 'Llantrisant' is appropriate at this point. The spelling of the place name with a single 'S' does not appear to have been standardised until late in the 19th century. The older 'Llantrissant' featured in the legal title of the L&TVJR and is therefore employed in this context throughout; elsewhere the modern 'Llantrisant' is used. Translated it means 'The church of the three saints'.

Llantrisant station looking towards Cardiff, *c*. 1910. The buildings on the down platform were provided for the joint use of the TVR and the GWR, as part of the rebuilding of 1889-1891.

Lens of Sutton

Station staff and others pose for the camera at Llantrisant, *c*. 1910.

Chapter One

Introduction

The valleys of the Rivers Taff and Ely, both of which reach the Bristol Channel at the Port of Cardiff, have provided natural routeways for successive forms of transport. Both were exploited early on in the development of the rail network of South Wales, and were to provide the basic framework for the complex system that emerged during the 19th century.

The intervening countryside is one of marked contrasts. The southern half forms part of the rolling Vale of Glamorgan, while the northern part comprises higher ground fragmented by a number of shallow valleys. Forming the dividing line between these two areas is a ridge of hills corresponding to the 'southern crop' of the South Wales coalfield. This ridge is cut through by both the Taff and the Ely, the former in spectacular fashion at Taffs Wells Gorge, the latter in a less dramatic manner to the west of Llantrisant. Other lesser streams, which drain the country to the north of the ridge, break through at Cross Inn, to the east of Llantrisant, and at Creigiau.

The town of Llantrisant occupies a dominant position, almost Mediterranean in character, astride a hill overlooking the Ely valley. An ancient market town, its charter having been granted by Hugh de Spencer in 1346, Llantrisant served a wide catchment area stretching up the Ely valley and into the Rhondda valleys. With the opening up of the Rhondda coalfield, however, Llantrisant was soon eclipsed as market centre by Pontypridd (known as Newbridge until 1843) at the confluence of the Rhondda and the Taff. To the east of Llantrisant were a number of small villages and hamlets, the most important being the village of Llantwit Fardre.

Llantrisant was also at the centre of mining activity from at least the 13th century. Significant exploitation of the haematite iron ore deposits to the south of the town, and of the household coal reserves to the north and east, did not, however, take place in earnest until about the middle of the 19th century. Geological conditions, combined with economic circumstances, meant that the subsequent development of the local mining industry was patchy and never approached the scale found elsewhere in the South Wales coalfield. Thus, at first sight, the prospects for the area, suffering as it did from generally unhelpful terrain and relatively uncertain traffic potential, did not appear especially enticing to railway speculators. Nevertheless, by the end of the 19th century, the area had been criss-crossed by a complex network of lines, both actual and projected. Today, the wheel has turned full circle, and the district between the South Wales Main Line and that of the former Taff Vale Railway has all but been erased from the railway map of South Wales.

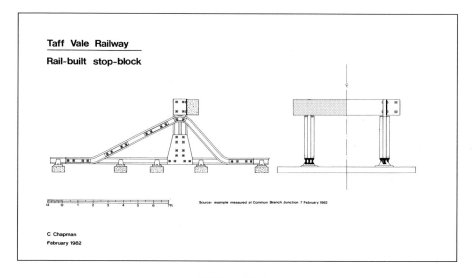

TVR stop block.

Detail of TVR permanent way materials.

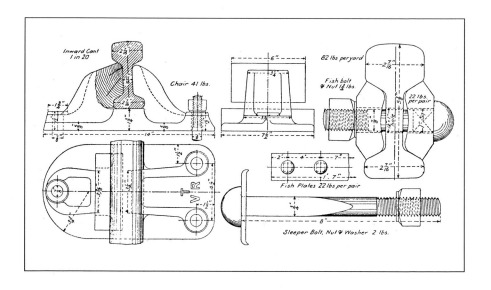

Chapter Two

Origins and Precursors

The development of the iron industry around Merthyr in the latter part of the 18th century gave rise to pressure for improved transport links to the coast. Until late in the century, such links were restricted to rough tracks across hilltop routes, over which the produce of the ironworks was conveyed on the backs of horses and mules. In 1771 an Act was passed for the creation of a turnpike road, via the Taff valley, from Merthyr to Tongwynlais, where it joined the Cardiff District Turnpike. This great advance was soon eclipsed, however, by the growth in demand and the accelerating pace of technological change. In 1784 a Bill was introduced for the construction of a canal from Merthyr to Cardiff. Although this attempt failed to reach the Statute Book, this proved only a temporary setback, for on 9th June, 1790 an Act was obtained incorporating the Glamorganshire Canal. The canal opened between Merthyr and Cardiff on 10th February, 1794.

Of particular note, in relation to later tramroad and railway developments, was the so-called 'Four Mile Clause' of the Glamorganshire Canal Act. This stated that 'proprietors of any mines, lying within 4 miles of any part of this canal, may make collateral cuts or railways across the grounds of any persons, on payment of damages'. The purpose of this clause, and of similar ones in other canal acts, was to enable branch canals, tramroads or railways to be taken from the canal without the need for further Parliamentary sanction. It also avoided the often exorbitant demands made by landowners in exchange for wayleaves.

The opening of the Glamorganshire Canal stimulated the growth of extractive and manufacturing industry along its route. One such development involved the easily accessible coal measures to the south of Treforest. By 1810 a tramroad had been laid from the canal, at Pont Maesmawr, to serve Maesbach Colliery, mid way between Treforest and Taffs Well. Constructed under the provisions of the 'Four Mile Clause', this tramroad crossed the River Taff at Upper Boat by means of a 'floating bridge', consisting of a ferry boat, on which one or two 'drams' were taken across the river between the two sections of tramroad. The boat was fitted with an adjustable framework which compensated for changes in river level, enabling the drams to be pushed on and off with ease on each side of the river.

In 1832 George Insole, owner of a shipping office in Cardiff from 1812 and later to become an important figure in the development of the coal industry of the Rhondda valleys, leased the mineral rights of the Maesbach Estate from the Revd J.T. Casberd. By this date, the colliery appears to have fallen into disuse, output having declined from over 15,000 tons in 1820 to 6,500 tons in 1830, with the name of its owner, J. Bennet Grover, disappearing from the returns of the Glamorganshire Canal Company in 1831. The following November Insole re-opened the Maesmawr level and sank a pit to the four feet seam, and in 1833 he purchased a steam forcing pump or 'working barrel' from the Neath Abbey

Ironworks, for use in this colliery.   By 1842 the enlarged operation was employing 157 men and boys, with its output having exceeded 23,000 tons in 1839.

With the continuing growth of the Merthyr iron industry, congestion on the Glamorganshire Canal soon became endemic. In 1823 plans were prepared for a railway or tramroad from the southern terminus of the historic Penydarren Tramroad, at Navigation House, near modern Abercynon, to Cardiff, along a route marked out by George Overton. From this 'main line' at Willowford, just south of Maesmawr, a branch line was to run, via Llantwit Fardre, to St John's Chapel, near Tonyrefail, with a further branch from this line to serve the town of Llantrisant. Not surprisingly, this scheme was fiercely opposed by the canal company, and was not taken any further.

Part of Overton's scheme re-emerged in 1829. On 23rd June, 1829 Robert Beaumont, mineral advisor to the Marquess of Bute, recommended that his Lordship make a 'railroad' to open up his mineral property at Llantrisant. The previous year, James Green, the eminent canal engineer, had prepared plans for a new dock at Cardiff, at the request of the Marquess. In September 1829, picking up where Beaumont had left off, Green prepared a report recommending that a 'railroad' be made from Cardiff to Llantrisant and St John's Chapel, along the lines earlier proposed by Overton.   Green also recommended that the line should be extended beyond St John's Chapel into the Rhondda Fawr valley and, by means of a tunnel at least 3 miles in length, on into the Vale of Neath. In the event, the Marquess was not persuaded by this ambitious scheme, and contented himself with building a dock at Cardiff, which opened on 9th October, 1839.

These early proposals foreshadowed the successful promotion of the Taff Vale Railway, from Merthyr to Cardiff. Incorporated by Act of 21st June, 1836, the TVR opened between Cardiff and Navigation House on 8th October, 1840, and from there to Merthyr on 21st April, 1841. The new railway passed close to the Maesmawr coal workings, but it was not until May 1846 that a siding to Insole's colliery was authorised, although it is not known if this was constructed.

Shortly before the TVR's Act of Incorporation, the proposal for lines to St John's Chapel and Llantrisant was brought up again. On 5th April, 1836 Beaumont wrote a memorandum to the Marquess of Bute setting out the general route of this proposal, which was to follow a similar line from Willowford to that proposed by Overton in 1823, a fact acknowledged in the memorandum. In a further memorandum, dated 24th October, 1836, the route was modified to leave the TVR at Maesmawr, where an inclined plane was to lift the line out of the Taff valley. At this stage, the TVR Board was giving consideration to matters to be included in a Bill for the 1837 Session of Parliament. In the event, any hopes that this would include provision for the St John's Chapel line proved ill-founded and the Bill confined itself to the acquisition of the Penydarren Tramroad, and the substitution of railway branches for junctions with various tramroads at Merthyr.

This was not the end of the Llantrisant scheme, however, for in September 1837 W.H. Harrison, Engineer, prepared a survey and plan of the proposed

lines for the Marquess of Bute. In addition to the lines to St John's Chapel and
Llantrisant, Harrison suggested the extension of the former into the Rhondda
Fawr and of the latter into the Ely valley to ward off the expansionist tendencies
of the Duffryn Llynvi and Porthcawl Railway! Despite these extensive
ambitions, however, Harrison was somewhat cautious regarding the initial
outlay, recommending only that the first four miles from Maesmawr be built.
An estimate was prepared of likely traffic, which included a modest sum for
passengers: 20 per day at 1 shilling each!

At the time of this proposal, it was reported that the first collieries were being
opened along the intended route, with others expected to follow. Foremost
among the coal speculators was Thomas Powell, one of the most important
pioneers in the development of the South Wales coalfield. Born in 1779, and
starting out as a timber merchant in Newport, Powell had entered the coal trade
about 1810. By 1840 he had become the major figure in the bituminous coal
trade of South Wales, owning four collieries in Monmouthshire and the eastern
edge of Glamorgan. The year before he had sent over 62,000 tons of coal down
the Glamorganshire Canal, a quarter of all the coal carried.

In 1837 Powell leased the mineral rights of Ystradbarwig Uchaf, west of
Llantwit Fardre, from Howell Jenkins. In November of that year Powell met E.P
Richards, agent to the Marquess of Bute, and agreed to join the Marquess in
promoting the 'Llantrissant Rail-road'. By February 1838, however, Powell was
expressing some dissatisfaction with Harrison's proposal. In particular, he felt
that the estimated cost of construction was too low, especially if, as he
proposed, a tunnel was substituted for the inclined plane at Maesmawr. Powell
then engaged his own surveyor to prepare a detailed plan and estimate, which
was put at £23,156 1s. 5d., of which Powell offered to advance £8,000.

Following this offer, the Marquess consulted Joseph Gray, another of his
mineral advisors, on the question of whether or not to build the railway. Gray
set out his conclusions in a lengthy report, dated 29th November, 1838. He
found that Harrison had over-estimated the cost of construction, partly by
proposing a haulage engine at the top of the incline, whereas it could easily be
worked on the balanced load principle. On the other hand, he was not
optimistic regarding traffic prospects, and concluded by noting that the
proposal was of a 'highly speculative nature and such that I cannot seek, or
know of sufficient inducement to recommend its adoption'. Faced with such a
conclusion, it is hardly surprising that the Marquess lost interest in this attempt
to promote a railway to Llantrisant.

This left Thomas Powell in something of a quandary, for if he was
successfully to exploit the coal reserves of the Llantwit Fardre district, he
needed an efficient transport link to the sea and the vital export trade. So, at the
end of 1842, he revived part of the earlier scheme to serve his new Dihewyd
Colliery, near Llantwit Fardre. In place of the junction with the TVR, however,
he proposed to take his railway to the Glamorganshire Canal. By so doing he
could take advantage of the Canal Act's 'Four Mile Clause', with all the savings
that would bring. There may also have been a second, more complex reason for
this apparent change of plan. Powell, as one of the original Directors of the
TVR, had been instrumental in getting that company to build its Llancaiach

branch, to serve his Gelligaer Colliery. In spite of this, however, he had fallen out with his fellow Directors, and continued to send his coal via the Glamorganshire Canal. He had sought a reduction in coal rates on his traffic and authority to use his own locomotive, neither of which the TVR was prepared to accede to. As this dispute was not resolved until the earlier part of 1843, it may well have influenced Powell's stated intention of taking his railway to the canal.

Powell's railway, variously known as the 'Lantwit Vardre Railway',* the 'Dihewyd Railway't and the 'Llantwit Branch', followed the route of the Marquess of Bute's earlier proposal to Maesmawr, where it occupied the course of a spur off the Maesmawr Tramroad for a short distance. It is not clear, however, if any physical use was ever made of the tramroad as a link between the Lantwit Vardre Railway and the canal. The 'connection' may simply have been a legal device in order to take advantage of the undoubted benefits of the 'Four Mile Clause'.

The Lantwit Vardre Railway was completed to Maesmawr by 28th December, 1843, when Powell appeared at the TVR Board demanding that a junction be made with the TVR 'without further delay'. In response, the Board ordered that an estimate be made of the cost of providing two sidings, each capable of holding 40 wagons. This estimate, amounting to £142 19s. 3d. per siding, generated some heat when it was presented to the Board on 9th January, 1844. Powell, with his customary eye to economy, offered to lay both sidings for a total sum of £180. The Board was not impressed, however, and resolved to lay only one siding, on the basis of the original estimate.

The connection between the Lantwit Vardre Railway and the TVR was opened to traffic on 25th April, 1844, when, in celebration of the occasion, a train of Powell's Llantwit coal was worked through to Cardiff. It was greeted along its route by general rejoicing, the display of flags and banners and the 'roar of small artillery'. A similar reception (but without the pyrotechnics) awaited the train on its arrival at the Cardiff terminus at 3.00 pm.

The junction at Maesmawr was facing to up trains, the TVR being single line at this point until doubled at the end of 1846. Shortly after leaving the main line, the Lantwit Vardre Railway turned through 90 degrees to the south-west, before ascending Maesmawr Incline. This was a self-acting inclined plane, worked on the balanced load principle, with a gradient of 1 in 6.6 and a length of 297 yards. From Incline Top, as it was known, the line followed a relatively level course to Dihewyd Colliery. Earthworks were negligible, with the only structure of any consequence being a small bridge over a brook, near Church Village.

The layout of the Lantwit Vardre Railway at Maesmawr soon gave rise to concern on grounds of safety. With its sharp bend at the foot of a very steep incline, it presented obvious dangers in the event of a 'wild run'. Having considered this problem, the TVR placed a sand bank at the foot of the incline to protect the main line. On 5th April, 1846, following a suggestion from Thomas Powell, instructions were given to replace this bank with a stone wall.

The opening of the Lantwit Fardre Railway appears to have drawn attention to the need for passenger facilities to serve the area to the west of Maesmawr.

* Referred to as such in the L&TVJR Act 1861

† Referred to as such in deposited plan for Lantwit Farder Railway 1847

A station at Maesmawr had opened on 30th October, 1840, but had not been successful and had closed on 20th April, 1841. On 1st April, 1845 'Memorials' from residents of the parishes of Llantrisant, Llantwit Fardre and Eglwyselin were presented to the TVR Board, seeking the provision of a station at the junction of the Lantwit Vardre Railway with the main line. In response, it was agreed, on an experimental basis, for arrangements to be made to book passengers at Maesmawr on Saturdays only.

This experiment was not a success; on 8th July, 1845 the TVR Board was informed that average receipts at Maesmawr 'station' for the 11 weeks from its opening had amounted to only 8 shillings (40p) per week for passengers and 2 shillings (10p) per week for goods. As a result, instructions were given to discontinue Maesmawr as a stopping place. This was not the end of the matter, however, for on 11th November, 1845 it was decided that on Sundays only trains should call at Maesmawr to pick up passengers. Just how long this practice was continued is not known, however.

In November 1847 a plan was deposited for a substantial diversion of the Lantwit Vardre Railway, together with its extension to Ystradbarwig Uchaf, to the west of Dihewyd Colliery. A new junction with the TVR, to the south of Maesmawr, was envisaged, with the Maesmawr Incline replaced by a more easily graded climb out of the Taff valley. Although this proposal went no further, the TVR responded to this desire for improvement on 11th January, 1848, when instructions were given 'to do whatever is necessary for accommodating Mr Powell's traffic'. In addition, authority was given to install a weighing machine for Powell's coal at Incline Top. The Lantwit Vardre Railway was subsequently extended to Ystradbarwig Colliery, but without recourse to Act of Parliament.

The town of Llantrisant acquired its first railway station, albeit in name only, on 18th June, 1850, when the South Wales Railway (SWR) opened between Chepstow and Swansea. Situated at Pontyclun, some two miles from Llantrisant, the station was a typical SWR wayside facility, with up and down platforms and a goods siding serving a goods shed and loading bank. The station building, on the up platform, was of characteristic 'Brunelian' style, with an overhanging hipped roof providing shelter on all sides. There was little in the way of settlement nearby at the opening of the station, but development soon followed, with the Windsor Hotel, adjoining the station, opening on 21st January, 1858.

Llantrisant station ('Llantrissant' until about 1890) acted as a railhead for a wide area, including the rural Vale of Glamorgan. In particular, it served the small market town of Cowbridge, about 5 miles to the south. On 6th December, 1855, a public meeting at Cowbridge agreed to promote a broad gauge railway from the town to Llantrisant station. The scale of this proposal soon expanded; on 25th March, 1856, the Provisional Committee of the 'Cowbridge and South Wales Junction Railway' announced its intention of continuing the line to Pontypridd. Following this, a survey was prepared and placed before a further public meeting at Cowbridge on 26th May, 1856. The line was to be 8¾ miles long, continuing beyond Pontypridd to Gyfeillion Colliery. The support of the SWR was sought, but in spite of the opportunity it afforded to penetrate the heart of TVR territory, the company was not prepared to back the Cowbridge scheme. Lacking sufficient local support, no further progress was made with the C&SWJR.

The failure of the C&SWJR coincided with the successful promotion of another broad gauge line from the SWR at Llantrisant station. On 4th October, 1856 a notice appeared in the *Cardiff and Merthyr Guardian*, announcing the formation of the 'Ely and Rhondda Valleys Railway Company'. By 12th November 1856, when the notice of its Bill was published for the 1857 Parliamentary Session, the scheme had been reduced to the more manageable proportions of the Ely Valley Railway (EVR). Incorporated by Act of 13th July, 1857, the EVR was promoted by various landowners and industrialists to tap the mineral wealth of the upper Ely valley, with branches to Glanmychydd (or Castellau) and Gellyrhaidd, near Hendreforgan. The first sod was cut with due ceremony at Llanelay Fach, near Pontyclun, on 17th May, 1858.

The ambitions of the EVR extended beyond the coal measures of the Ely valley. On 14th June, 1858 an Act was obtained for a branch from the main line to Mwyndy and Broviskin. The object of this branch was the haematite iron ore deposits of the Mwyndy district, to the south-east of Llantrisant. Ore had been mined here from at least the 13th century, but its real development came in the 1850s. The Bute Iron Ore Mine re-opened on 22nd October, 1852, followed by the opening of the Mwyndy Iron Ore Mine in May 1855. In 1856 the Mwyndy mine was acquired by N.E. Vaughan of Llanely Hall, near Pontyclun. Vaughan was one of the prime movers behind the promotion of the EVR. The key factor that encouraged the development of the Mwyndy iron ore deposits was the increase in the cost of local coalfield ironstone. By the 1850s it was becoming cheaper to import haematite ore from such places as Furness and West Cumberland, rather than to use local ironstone.

Unfortunately, the Mwyndy mines were at a competitive disadvantage, owing to the high cost of transport to the ironworks of the northern fringes of Glamorgan and Monmouthshire. The opening of the Mwyndy branch of the EVR by February 1859, albeit with temporary track and worked by horses, provided rail access, but did little to overcome this basic handicap. The route from the iron ore mines to the works was circuitous, in any event, but as the EVR had been built to the broad gauge, transport required costly transhipment at break of gauge and a lengthy detour, via Neath and the Vale of Neath Railway, to Merthyr.

The inherent disadvantages of the broad gauge also applied in the case of coal traffic. The main markets for the bituminous coal of the Ely valley were the same iron works, all of which were on the 'narrow' (i.e. standard) gauge. In addition, the export trade was handicapped by the very limited provision made for broad gauge traffic at Cardiff Docks.

The opportunities presented by these shortcomings soon attracted the attention of another local company. On 15th December, 1858 the Directors of the Penarth Harbour Dock and Railway Company (PHD&R) agreed to approach the EVR, with a view to forging a standard gauge link between the two railways. The PHD&R had been incorporated as the Ely Tidal Harbour and Railway by Act of 21st July, 1856, the change of name and construction of a dock being sanctioned by a further Act on 27th July, 1857. In December 1858 construction of the harbour and railway to the TVR, at Radyr, was nearing completion, the undertaking being opened on 18th July, 1859.

On 18th January, 1859 a PHD&R deputation appeared before the EVR Board, with a proposition for connecting the two railways. This could either take the form of a junction between the PHD&R and the SWR, with mixed gauge over the SWR, or an independent standard gauge line from the EVR to the PHD&R. In either case, the EVR would convert to standard gauge. Having considered this approach, the EVR Directors resolved, on 22nd February, 1859, that it was desirable for their railway to be converted to standard gauge and to be linked to the PHD&R. They also felt that this was a useful opportunity to conclude a traffic arrangements with the SWR. The preferred form of connection between the EVR and the PHD&R was by means of the mixed gauge over the SWR, with a junction between that line and the PHD&R, and running powers granted to the EVR. Accordingly, a deputation was appointed to deal with both the SWR and the PHD&R.

At first the SWR responded positively to this suggestion. On 9th June, 1859 the EVR Board was informed that the SWR welcomed the proposal, and was prepared to lay the necessary third rail. On becoming aware of this situation, however, the GWR (which leased and worked the SWR) intervened and vetoed any agreement. A subsequent attempt to persuade the SWR to lease or purchase the EVR failed to illicit a response. In the wake of these rebuffs, the need for an independent link to the PHD&R became pressing, and in November 1859 plans were deposited for an extension of the Mwyndy branch to join the PHD&R. In addition, powers were sought for an east-west curve at Mwyndy Junction, together with extensions from Penrhiwfer to Penygraig, and from Gellyrhaidd to Gilfach Goch and Blackmill.

Negotiations with the PHD&R appeared to be making good progress, with agreement in sight, when, on 8th March, 1860, the EVR suddenly decided to abandon its proposed connection to the PHD&R. The reasons given, at the time, for this decision were the limited development of the coal reserves of the Ely valley and the poor financial position of the company. In its report to its shareholders of 23rd August, 1860, however, the company stated that the scheme had been withdrawn on account of the opposition it had aroused. The source of this opposition is not hard to discern. On 27th June, 1860, following an approach from the GWR to lease or purchase its undertaking, the EVR Board enthusiastically agreed to enter into negotiations with that company. The GWR's motives for this move are revealed in a letter, dated 10th December, 1860, from Daniel Gooch, in which he stated that 'our object in taking the line would be chiefly for getting a connection to our colliery' (i.e. Gyfeillion, near Pontypridd). Terms were agreed in February 1861, the lease of the EVR being operative from 1st January, 1861, and confirmed by Act of 29th July, 1862. It was not until 1903, however, that the EVR was formally amalgamated with the GWR.

Meanwhile, work was progressing with the construction of the EVR. On 7th February, 1860 the EVR Board was informed that the temporary track on the Mwyndy branch had been replaced with the permanent variety. This was followed, on 2nd August, 1860, by the opening of the main line from Llantrisant to Penrhiwfer, accompanied by the usual celebrations, a special train conveying the Directors and officers of the EVR to the event.

The lease by the GWR provided financial salvation for the Ely Valley Company, especially as its traffic was proving very slow to develop. It did nothing, however, to alter the basic problem faced by the company, namely its isolation from the main markets for the produce of the area it served.

Thus, by the middle of 1860, the country between Llantrisant and the Taff valley had been penetrated by rail on two fronts: by the Mwyndy branch of the EVR, and by the Lantwit Vardre Railway from the TVR to Ystradbarwig Colliery. Extension of the EVR towards Llantwit Fardre appears to have been considered, but rejected for fear of TVR opposition. An extension of the Castellau branch to Pontypridd also appears to have been considered. Nevertheless, if a standard gauge line could be made between these somewhat incompatible railheads, a number of possibilities would be opened up. These included the more extensive development of the Llantwit coalfield, the creation of a direct route between the Mwyndy iron ore mines and their markets, and the prospect of standard gauge advancement into the areas to the south and west of Llantrisant. In September 1860 these opportunities awaited recognition and exploitation.

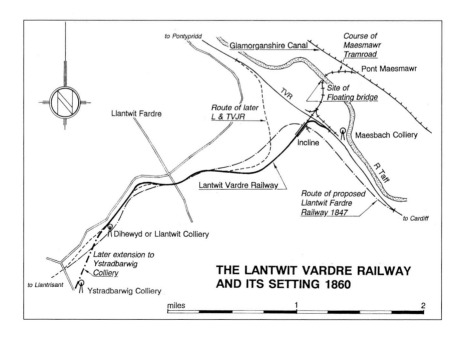

THE LANTWIT VARDRE RAILWAY
AND ITS SETTING 1860

The Llantrissant and Taff Vale Junction Railway Promotion and Construction 1860-1865

Recognition of the opportunities presented by the fragmented nature of the railway system of Llantrisant and Llantwit Fardre came from an unexpected source. On 12th September, 1860 a Merthyr solicitor, W. Simons, appeared before the TVR Board with a proposition. Simons, partner in the firm of Simons and Evans, had conceived a scheme for connecting the Mwyndy iron ore field with the TVR. He informed the TVR Directors that he had acquired Powell's Lantwit Vardre Railway for £9,000, and was prepared to incorporate this asset in a standard gauge line to be projected from Llantrisant to the TVR. For this he sought a premium on his purchase and appointment as solicitor to the company to be formed to carry out his scheme. He had prepared a draft prospectus and estimate of cost, which he put at £30,000.

The TVR Board did not make an immediate response, however, but instructed its general superintendent, George Fisher, to undertake a survey of the Lantwit Vardre Railway and to investigate the traffic potential of Simons' proposal. At the same time, William Done Bushell, the company's Resident Director (i.e. managing director) was to contact the iron ore companies to ascertain what interest they would take in the proposed railway.

Fisher completed his report on 2nd October, 1860. He had come to the view that while it was not necessary, from an engineering point of view, to make use of the Lantwit Vardre Railway, there could well be a financial case for doing so. He had prepared a plan for the extension of the Lantwit Vardre Railway to Llantrisant. Fisher's plan also showed a continuation from Llantrisant to Cowbridge, to be made by 'another company'. He felt that although it would be practicable to replace Maesmawr Incline with a locomotive-worked gradient of 1 in 40, without any material departure from the junction of the Lantwit Vardre Railway with the TVR, a much better alignment could be obtained by making a new junction, about ½ mile to the north. With this alteration, only about 1¼ mile of the Lantwit Vardre Railway would need to be made use of. Fisher put the cost of the new railway at £30,000. He could see good traffic prospects in the case of iron ore, with the Llantwit coal reserves, although much faulted, also providing a worthwhile source of revenue.

Having considered Fisher's report at their meeting on 3rd October, 1860, the TVR Directors resolved to subscribe £10,000 towards a new company, the 'Llantrissant and Taff Vale Junction Railway' (L&TVJR), to be formed to implement Simons' proposal. A prospectus for the new company was published on 16th October, 1860. In it great play was made of the savings that would be made in the cost of carrying Mwyndy iron ore to the iron works of Merthyr and the heads of the valleys. Dramatic reductions in mileages would result with the completion of the railway: Mwyndy to Merthyr, for example, would be only 19 miles, compared with 54 miles by the old broad gauge route, via Neath. The new railway would also provide a standard gauge route from Llantrisant and Llantwit Fardre to the docks at Cardiff and Penarth. It would

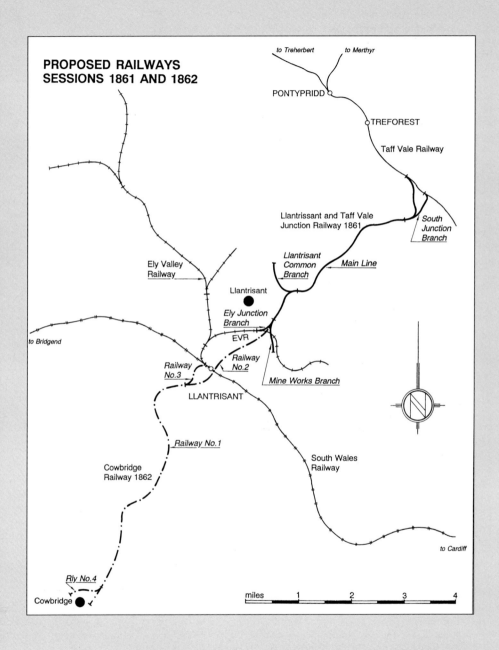

PROPOSED RAILWAYS
SESSIONS 1861 AND 1862

to Treherbert   to Merthyr

PONTYPRIDD

TREFOREST

Taff Vale Railway

Llantrissant and Taff Vale
Junction Railway 1861

South
Junction
Branch

Ely Valley
Railway

Llantrisant
Common
Branch

Main Line

Llantrisant

Ely Junction
Branch

to Bridgend

EVR

Railway
No.3

Railway
No.2

LLANTRISANT

Mine Works Branch

Railway No.1

Cowbridge
Railway 1862

South Wales
Railway

to Cardiff

Rly No.4

Cowbridge

miles   1   2   3   4

impinge upon the property of only two landowners, both of whom were expected to accept shares in lieu of payment for their land.

Simons had other ambitions beyond the promotion of the L&TVJR. While the TVR Board was considering his proposal, he had met R.C. Nichol-Carne, Mayor of Cowbridge, and put forward the suggestion that an independent company should be formed to link that town with the L&TVJR. Nichol-Carne responded enthusiastically to this idea, and, on 27th September, 1860, a public meeting was held at Cowbridge to discuss the proposal. Simons' involvement in the promotion of the Cowbridge Railway came to an abrupt and unceremonious end, however, when, on 23rd October, 1860, a second public meeting decided that the railway to Cowbridge should be built by the TVR, something that company was clearly not prepared to do.

Simons' fortunes fared little better with the promotion of the L&TVJR. On examining Powell's titles to the land occupied by his railway, the TVR soon found them to be defective, thereby making Simons' claim to ownership invalid. When direct negotiations between Powell and the TVR failed, plans were prepared for an independent line for the L&TVJR. It was, however, thought prudent to include the Lantwit Vardre Railway within the 'limits of deviation' shown on the Deposited Plans, so that it could still, if necessary, be incorporated in the L&TVJR. To allow for this change of plan, the company's capital requirement was increased to £40,000, of which one third was to be subscribed by the TVR.

Up to this point, Simons had acted as solicitor to the L&TVJR. With the emergence of these difficulties, however, he was asked to resign, as to have retained him would have been 'fruitful of difficulties', according to the L&TVJR record. With this rebuff and compensation of £500, Simons' involvement in the promotion of the L&TVJR ceased.

In November 1860 plans were deposited for the L&TVJR. A total of five railways were proposed, including the 'Main Line' from the TVR to Cross Inn, near Llantrisant, the 'Ely Junction branch' from Cross Inn to a junction with the EVR, the 'Mine Works branch' to serve the Bute Iron Ore Mine, the 'Common branch' from Cross Inn into Llantrisant Common, and the 'South Junction branch', closely paralleling Powell's railway at Maesmawr Incline.

The L&TVJR Bill was opposed by Thomas Powell and the EVR. During examination before the House of Commons Committee, it emerged that the South Junction branch was simply a device to safeguard the company in the event of it wishing to acquire the whole of the Lantwit Vardre Railway. The Committee recommended the deletion of this branch, but granted power for the purchase of the Lantwit Vardre Railway, but by agreement rather than compulsion. After the Bill had passed through Committee stage, Powell put forward a fresh proposal for the sale of his railway, which proved acceptable to the L&TVJR, agreement being made on 23rd May, 1861.

Having considered the EVR's objections, the Committee recommended that the Mine Works branch be struck out, to be replaced by the provision of a third rail from the junction between the EVR and the L&TVJR (henceforth Maesaraul Junction) to the 'south-eastern terminus' of the Mwyndy branch, together with the grant of running powers over this section. The TVR eventually obtained running powers, as agent for the Cowbridge Railway, between Llantrisant and Maesaraul Junction, as a result of an agreement between the Cowbridge Company and the GWR, as lessees of the EVR, dated 9th January, 1864.

The L&TVJR was incorporated by Act of 7th June, 1861. The Act authorised the purchase of the Lantwit Vardre Railway, together with its alteration and extension, and provided for the grant of running powers over part of the Mwyndy branch of the EVR. It also empowered the TVR to subscribe towards the undertaking, to vote at meetings, and to enter into working and traffic agreements with the new company. Capital of the L&TVJR was set at £40,000, with borrowing powers at £13,000. Five years were allowed for completion. The first Directors were James Poole, Chairman of the TVR, and W. Done Bushell, E.H. Lee and H.J. Evans, all Directors of that company. Despite its legal status as an independent company, for most practical purposes the L&TVJR functioned as an integral part of the TVR. In addition to sharing Directors, it also enjoyed the services of TVR officers, with George Fisher acting as Engineer and Frederick Marwood as Secretary.

With the Parliamentary struggle behind it, the company's first general meeting, on 22nd August, 1861, was an occasion for self-congratulation and renewed commitment to the early completion of the railway. The meeting was asked to support the Board's recommendation that a fifth Director, Dr J.W. Nichol-Carne of Dimlands, near Llantwit Major, be added to their number. This having been agreed, the meeting was informed that Powell's railway had been acquired, and that steps had been taken to obtain possession of land for the new section of railway between the TVR and the Lantwit Vardre Railway. Contracts for the construction of this section were to be entered into without delay, whilst no time was to be lost in serving notices for the rest of the land needed for the railway. The next important step took place on 12th September, 1861, when the Directors accepted Ambrose Oliver's tender for constructing the railway.

The question of running powers over the Mwyndy branch became the subject of dispute between the L&TVJR and the EVR in August 1861. Although the L&TVJR Act referred to running powers to its 'south-eastern terminus', the Mwyndy branch had been extended a further ¼ mile since the passing of that Act. The EVR argued that the 'south-eastern terminus' was, in fact, the terminus of the branch at the time of the passing of the Act, whereas the L&TVJR considered it to be the actual terminus. This dispute dragged on until April 1863, when Counsel's opinion was sought. Counsel J.H. Lloyd took the view that the 'south-eastern terminus' was that shown on the deposited plans for the Mwyndy branch of 1857. In the light of this the EVR relented and the L&TVJR agreed to pay tolls in respect of the actual distance travelled by its trains over the branch. The terms and conditions relating to running powers and the laying of the third rail over the Mwyndy branch were finalised in an agreement between the L&TVJR and the GWR, dated 9th January, 1864.

By the time of the second half-yearly report on 14th February, 1862, encouraging progress had been made with the construction of the L&TVJR. Work on the connecting section between the TVR and the Lantwit Vardre Railway was well advanced, and land had been acquired for improving the existing railway between Tonteg and Llantwit Fardre. The Directors were optimistic that coal would be conveyed over the new railway in the following July. The remaining sections of the L&TVJR were still only at a preparatory stage, however, although property plans had been prepared and notices served on landowners.

The pace of this initial burst of activity was not maintained, however. Reporting on the situation on 9th August, 1862, George Fisher noted that work had been retarded by inclement weather and delays in obtaining possession of land. Nevertheless, he remained hopeful that the section from the TVR to Powell's Llantwit collieries would be completed within the month. The weather continued its unkind course, however, and it was not until 6th February, 1863 that Fisher was able to report the 'completion' of this section of the railway, together with siding accommodation at the junction with the TVR. The sections to the west of Llantwit Fardre were progressing as rapidly as the weather permitted. In the event, expectations of the imminent opening of the line as far as Llantwit collieries proved somewhat premature, for on 6th May, 1863 the L&TVJR Board was informed that Ambrose Oliver, the contractor, was in financial difficulties and had ceased work. Faced with this setback, it was resolved that the company should complete the work itself, although on 24th June, 1863, it was reported that the contract had been relet to J.E. Billups, a contractor responsible for a great deal of work on the TVR.

With work restarted, Fisher felt confident enough to announce, in the fifth half-yearly report to shareholders on 7th August, 1863, that the line was 'sufficiently forward' to be opened as far as the Llantwit collieries on 1st September, 1863. Fisher's prediction proved slightly inaccurate, however, as it was not until 17th September that the first section of the L&TVJR, from the TVR at Llantrisant Junction to the Llantwit collieries, was opened for the conveyance of coal. Powell himself did not live to see the opening; he died on 24th March, 1863, aged 89 years, having been at his desk in his Newport office until the previous day. Under the terms of his will, Powell's mineral property passed to his three sons. Of these, Thomas Powell Jnr soon gave up his interest in the firm's steam coal collieries to concentrate on Llantwit house coal collieries. The remainder of the business was acquired from Walter and Henry Powell, for £365,000, by George Elliot, the Northumberland mining engineer who had been brought in to value the assets of the company. On 28th July, 1864 the 'Powell Duffryn Steam Coal Co.' was formed to work the steam coal collieries.

The opening of this first section brought welcome traffic to the railway. Attainment of the main objective, the Mwyndy iron ore, was, however, dependant on the completion of the line through to Maesaraul Junction, together with the laying of the third rail from there to Broviskin. Naturally, the iron ore companies were anxious to see this achieved at the earliest opportunity. In October 1863 the Mwyndy Iron Ore Company demanded to know when this opening would take place, to which the L&TVJR Board replied that it was hoped it would be within two months. This proved the case as far as the section to Maesaraul Junction was concerned: by 29th January, 1864 the line had been opened as far as Thomas Powell Jnr's new colliery to the west of Llantwit, and on to Llantwit Dynevor Colliery and Cross Inn, just short of Maesaraul Junction. This was of little use to the iron ore companies, however, without the provision of the third rail over the Mwyndy branch. This was dependent on the GWR, which, despite its undertaking to lay the third rail within three months of the agreement with the L&TVJR of 9th January, 1864, showed no great urgency in carrying out its obligation. Indeed, it was not until two months after this date that instructions were given to carry out the necessary work. A month later, on 29th April, 1864, George Fisher was moved to comment on the slowness with which the GWR Engineer was progressing with the work. Matters did not improve, and on 12th August, 1864 the L&TVJR Board was informed that notice had been served on the GWR requiring the laying of the third rail. Delays continued, however, to the increasing annoyance of the L&TVJR. Macdermot gives the opening date of the mixed gauge over the Mwyndy branch as 5th December, 1864, but it would appear that iron ore was conveyed over the L&TVJR prior to that date, as on 22nd September, 1864 the TVR Board considered a request from the Mwyndy Iron Ore Co. for a reduction in tolls on its iron ore. This was agreed, the reduction being effective from 1st October, 1864.

Work on the Common branch did not start until some time after that on the L&TVJR main line. On 24th November, 1863, in response to a request from the promoter of a colliery at Gelynog, near Beddau, the L&TVJR agreed to construct the branch, provided the colliery promoter agreed to sink his colliery at the same time, and lay a private siding to connect with the Common branch. There was some delay in acquiring the necessary land, but in August 1864 L&TVJR Chairman James Poole, was able to report that the branch was nearly ready for traffic.

The construction of the L&TVJR gave a powerful stimulus to the development of the Llantwit Fardre coalfield. On 15th August, 1863 about 250 workmen were treated to a dinner in celebration of the winning of coal at Powell and Son's new Tynant Colliery, near Beddau. In the following January the *Cardiff Times* reported that the colliery was turning out a 'large quantity of the very best quality of household and gas coal'. In addition, a branch railway was being made to the Llantwit Wallsend Colliery, midway between Llantwit Fardre and Llantrisant, and Llantwit Dynevor Colliery, near Cross Inn, was being resuscitated. Thomas Powell Jnr was also active on Llantrisant Common, to the north of the town, and on 27th October, 1865, it was reported that coal had been won at his new colliery. In sinking this colliery, however, Powell had encroached on the common in infringement of the rights of the Burgesses of Llantrisant. On 6th April, 1866 it was reported that the Burgesses had entered Powell's colliery and forcibly stopped work. Nevertheless work continued, with the first train of coal being sent over the new private line to the Common branch of the L&TVJR on 30th July, 1866. In the event, however, the colliery was not as productive as expected owing to the presence of a fault, and working proved short lived. Nearby, another short-lived colliery had been opened on Llwyncrwn Farm by the Llantwit Main Colliery Co. The following March this company was said to be on the verge of selling out to Thomas Powell Jnr.

Powell's activities in the area were cut short, however, for in 1869 he was killed while travelling in what is now Ethiopia. He was buried on 5th November, 1869, Tynant Colliery coming to a stand for the day, as a mark of respect. Following Powell's death, his Llantwit collieries passed to the new ownership under the title of 'Powell's Llantwit Colliery Co.' This went into voluntary liquidation in 1876.

The opening up of the mineral wealth of the area attracted interest from a most surprising source. In November 1863 the Brecon and Merthyr Railway deposited plans for a railway from its line, north of Caerphilly, to a junction with the L&TVJR, just south of Llantrisant Junction. The object of this proposal was to provide an alternative route for coal and iron ore to the heads of the valleys, but the line was struck out in Committee, during the passage of the Bill.

After the false start in October 1860, the Cowbridge Railway was successfully promoted as an independent company, with the TVR agreeing to subscribe up to £5,000 towards the undertaking. Incorporated by Act of 29th July, 1862, the company was to build a standard gauge railway from Cowbridge to the L&TVJR at Maesaraul Junction, with a short spur to Llantrisant station, for exchange of goods traffic with the SWR. This arrangement was abandoned however, following agreement with the GWR, dated 9th January, 1864, under which accommodation for the standard gauge was to be provided between Llantrisant station and Maesaraul Junction, with running powers granted to the Cowbridge Company over this section.

Work on the Cowbridge Railway started in June 1863. It was to be served by a passenger train service from Pontypridd, passing over the L&TVJR en route, and provided by the TVR, which was to supply locomotive, rolling stock and train crew at cost price. The Cowbridge Railway was inspected by Colonel Yolland for the Board of Trade, on 17th December, 1864, but sanction was withheld because of a number of unacceptable features in its design and construction. At that stage the L&TVJR and the connecting section of the EVR were not ready for inspection. Notice of intention to open the L&TVJR to passengers was forwarded to the Board of Trade on 23rd December, 1864, but was withdrawn six days later owing to the incompleteness of the works. By 16th January, 1865, however, things were sufficiently advanced for a light engine to work through to Cowbridge, and on 30th January, 1865 a special goods train, loaded with Powell's Llantwit coal, ran through to the town to mark the opening of the Cowbridge Railway. Regular goods trains commenced on 8th February, 1865, running between Cowbridge and Maesaraul Junction, where exchange of traffic took place.

The various lines between Llantrisant Junction and Cowbridge were inspected by Captain Rich for the Board of Trade on 22nd March, 1865. Captain Rich travelled by the 9.25 am train from Cardiff to Merthyr, which made a special stop at Llantrisant Junction, where he was met by W. Done Bushell, George Fisher and B. Matthews, the L&TVJR solicitor, together with other gentlemen connected with the new railway. The party then transferred to 'an elegant first class carriage' for the journey to Llantrisant and Cowbridge.

In his report of inspection, Captain Rich noted with respect to the L&TVJR, that:

The new line is 4 miles 72 chains long and is single with sidings. Land has been purchased for a double line. The gauge is 4 feet 8½ inches. The rail used is double-headed in length of 21 feet and weighs 73 lbs per lineal yard. It is fished and fixed in joint chairs weighing 31 lbs and intervening chairs weigh 24 lbs each with compressed chairs driven inside the rail.

The fishplates are fastened with cotters instead of nuts and the chairs are bolted to sleepers 9 feet long by 2½ inches laid transversely about 3 feet 3 inches apart. A bridge rail is laid on the underbridges. The line is well-ballasted and in good order.

There are no stations and no public level crossings.

There are three over and nine under bridges built of stone. These works appear substantially constructed and of sufficient strength.

The gradients are steep. The approaches to the junctions at either end are on 1 in 40. At the Taff Vale end the new line runs for about 300 yards alongside the Taff Vale Railway on the level before it joins and there are no facing points at this junction as the connection with the down line is formed by a cross-over to the up line. I am of opinion that an ordinary double junction with locked points and signals would be better and Mr Fisher has agreed to substitute it.

The junction with the Ely Valley Railway is at the bottom of an incline of 1 in 40 close to an over bridge. It should be moved approximately 300 yards south from the over bridge. The points and signals should be properly connected and the levers placed in a raised box for the signalman.

The line is in good order and might be opened for passenger traffic were it not that the junction with the Mwyndy Branch of the Ely Valley Railway is incomplete. Consequently, there is no station at which passengers can be deposited or transferred.

In the light of these defects, Rich recommended that sanction should not be granted for the use of the new railway by passenger trains. He was, however, satisfied with the alterations which had been carried out on the Cowbridge Railway.

Matters were further delayed as a result of a dispute between the L&TVJR and the GWR concerning responsibility for carrying out the alterations required at Maesaraul Junction. Consequently, it was not until 14th August, 1865 that the L&TVJR was able to request a re-inspection of the railway. This was carried out by Captain Rich, who reported, on 29th August, 1865, that the hitherto incomplete works were in a fit state for passenger traffic.

Chapter Four

The L&TVJR Main Line
1865-1889

With the hurdle of Board of Trade approval removed, the passenger train service over the L&TVJR could, at last, begin. The main object of this service was, of course, to provide a link between the Cowbridge Railway and Pontypridd (which the TVR continued to call 'Newbridge' until late in 1865), a role which was emphasised by the complete absence of stations on the L&TVJR itself. The service commenced on 18th September, 1865, the *Cardiff Times* reporting that 'it was opened without any ceremony or display, the pioneer engine being simply decked with evergreens'. With only two trains each way and no intermediate stations between Llantrisant and Treforest, however, the benefits of the new service to local residents were decidedly limited. This state of affairs soon gave rise to adverse comment. On 22nd September, 1865 a correspondent to the *Cardiff Times* suggested that a station should be provided at Church Village, while an editorial in the same paper, on 29th September, 1865, pressed for stations at Church Village and near Llantrisant. In November 1865 a memorial, seeking a station at Maesaraul Junction, and signed by tradesmen and inhabitants of the town and neighbourhood of Llantrisant, was presented to the TVR Board.

The TVR was well aware of these shortcomings, however, as shortly after the introduction of the passenger train service George Fisher had advocated the provision of stations to serve Llantwit Fardre and Llantrisant. He had also proposed that an interchange station should be built at Llantrisant Junction, so that Llantrisant trains could be kept clear of the TVR main line. Although these recommendations were accepted by the TVR Board on 22nd September, 1865, no evidence has been found to suggest that such an interchange station was ever provided.

It was not until October 1866 that work on Llantwit station actually started. The new station, close to the site of Thomas Powell's Dihewyd Colliery, was opened by January 1867, when it made its first appearance in the public timetable. The town of Llantrisant, however, still lacked a convenient station. Its inhabitants were becoming increasingly restive at the sight of passenger trains to Pontypridd passing close to their town, whilst they themselves were faced with a two mile walk - in the wrong direction - to the GWR station. On 11th May, 1869 a public meeting was held at Llantrisant Town Hall to press for a more convenient station and an improved train service. Following this meeting, a deputation attended the TVR Board, on 28th May, 1869, with a request for a station to be built at Maesaraul Junction. This was received favourably but, in the event, a site at Cross Inn, to the east of Llantrisant, was selected for the new station. Start of work on the new station was reported on 24th July, 1869 and on 6th September, 1869 Cross Inn station was opened to passengers, the *Cardiff Times* noting that 'a great many people availed themselves of the convenience'. The inaugural service comprised only two trains, each way, but this was increased to three the following September, with

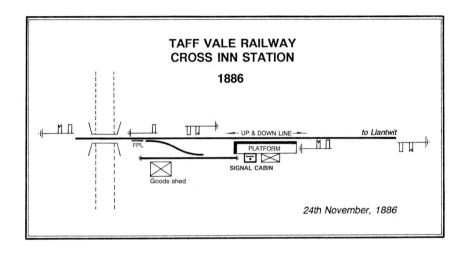

In the days before the growth of motorised traffic, the camera attracts attention at Cross Inn.   *C. Chapman Collection*

the introduction of a mid-morning departure from Cowbridge (11.00 am from Llantrisant), returning from Pontypridd at noon.

It is clear from contemporary accounts that, at the time of its opening in 1865, there was a general expectation that it was only a matter of time before the Cowbridge Railway was either leased to or purchased by the TVR. Relations between the two companies soon deteriorated, however, so much so that in August 1866 the TVR, having refused to enter into a permanent working agreement with the Cowbridge Company, went so far as to offer its assistance in seeking an alternative arrangement with the GWR. This indifference on the part of the TVR stemmed from the poor performance of the Cowbridge Railway, with its very limited contribution to the traffic of the larger company. The Cowbridge Railway had been under-capitalised from the start, so that its standard of construction left much to be desired. With maintenance almost non-existent, its permanent way soon began to deteriorate, much to the concern of the TVR, as provider of the locomotive and rolling stock used on the railway. As a result, on 22nd January, 1869, the TVR issued an ultimatum to the effect that it would withdraw its engine and carriages unless the Cowbridge Railway was put in good order. Although this particular threat was averted, as a result of the action of a group of Cowbridge freight forwarders in volunteering the labour needed to repair the line, the underlying problems remained. Following a further rejection of its request that the TVR lease, purchase or work its railway, the Cowbridge Company decided to go its own way, and gave notice to the TVR to withdraw its engine and rolling stock, as from 4th April, 1870.

This decision had serious implications for the operation of the passenger train service over the L&TVJR. The TVR itself did not have running powers over the EVR between Maesaraul Junction and Llantrisant station; it simply acted as agent for the Cowbridge Company. According to George Fisher, writing on 21st May 1870, the TVR would have been content to have terminated its trains from Pontypridd at Maesaraul Junction, connecting there with Cowbridge trains. He had to acknowledge, however, that the TVR did not possess the land needed for a station at the junction, whilst the Cowbridge Railway, of course, lacked the resources necessary for such a service. As a result, the two companies agreed, albeit as a 'temporary expedient', that the TVR would continue to work its trains through to Llantrisant station, and pay rental of £200 pa to the GWR for the use of the Maesaraul Junction - Llantrisant section. At first the TVR resisted demands for it to pay a proportion of the station and junction expenses at Llantrisant, but in December 1871, it reluctantly agreed to pay £70 pa as its contribution towards these costs.

Under its Act of 20th June, 1870 the L&TVJR was empowered to lease its undertaking to the TVR for 999 years from the opening of the railway for public use. With the passing of this Act the independence of the L&TVJR became, for most practical purposes. purely nominal.

The end of the broad gauge in South Wales in 1872 saw the removal of the third rail on the Mwyndy branch of the EVR, and did away with the need for transhipment at Llantrisant station. The EVR lines were kept open to broad gauge traffic until Saturday 11th May, 1872, conversion to standard gauge being completed over the weekend. One consequence of the gauge conversion was

Pontypridd-Llantrisant Timetable
July 1875

Pontypridd	dep.	8.44 am	11.40 am	7.28 pm	
Llantrisant	arr.	9.15	12.14 pm	8.05	
Connection					
for Cowbridge	dep.	9.25	12.20	8.10	
Cowbridge	arr.	9.50	12.45	8.35	

				TX	TO
Cowbridge	dep.	7.30 am		4.55 pm	5.50 pm
Connection					
from Cowbridge	arr.	7.50		5.20	6.10
Llantrisant	dep.	8.00	10.45 am	6.20	6.20
Pontypridd	arr.	8.32	11.21	6.57	6.57

Pontypridd-Llantrisant Timetable
September 1876

Pontypridd	dep.	8.44 am	11.42 am	7.34 pm
Treforest	dep.	8.48	11.46	7.39
Llantwit	dep.	9.00	12.00	7.54
Cross Inn	dep.	9.07	12.07 pm	8.02
Llantrisant	arr.	9.15	12.16	8.11
Cowbridge	arr.	9.46	12.45	8.38

Cowbridge	dep.	7.30 am	10.15 am	5.00 pm
Llantrisant	dep.	8.00	10.45	6.20
Cross Inn	dep.	8.08	10.55	6.30
Llantwit	dep.	8.15	11.02	6.37
Treforest	dep.	8.28	11.17	6.53
Pontypridd	arr.	8.32	11.21	6.57

TX   except Tuesdays.
TO   Tuesdays only.

the removal of the points at Mwyndy Juction. As a result the main Ely Valley line and the Mwyndy branch ran as parallel single lines from their convergence, at the site of Mwyndy Junction to Llantrisant station. In 1874 connections were installed at Mwyndy Junction which enabled this section to be worked as a conventional double line.

There was significant growth in iron ore traffic in the early 1870s, with the Bute and Mwyndy mines producing over 400,000 tons between 1870 and 1875. Output declined after 1875, but in 1878 the Mwyndy Iron Ore Co. opened Trecastle Mine, near Llanharry, on the Cowbridge Railway. This brought more iron ore to the L&TVJR, just at the time that traffic from the Bute and Mwyndy mines was starting to decline.

Coal traffic also benefited from the opening of a number of new mines. By 1876 the Llest Llantwit Colliery, near Llantwit station, was in production, together with Rica Colliery, on the site of Thomas Powell's earlier Dihewyd Colliery. None were to achieve long life, however, and by the end of the decade the coalfield was largely dormant.

After its break with the TVR in 1870, the Cowbridge Railway struggled on for over five years, in increasing financial difficulties and physical decrepitude. In March 1875 things came to a head: faced with the prospect of closure, the Cowbridge Company was forced to go cap in hand to the TVR for help. In these circumstances the TVR was able to dictate its own terms and, on 4th May, 1875 a meeting of Cowbridge shareholders accepted the TVR's terms for the lease of their railway. Following a thorough rehabilitation of the Cowbridge line, through working between Pontypridd and Cowbridge was restored.

In September 1875 a new method of reversing Llantrisant branch trains at Pontypridd was introduced. This involved the empty trains being turned via Pontypridd North Curve, opened to goods traffic in October 1872. This greatly simplified train working at the increasingly congested station, although, in the absence of a trailing crossover on the Merthyr line at Northern Junction, empty stock had to be propelled 'wrong line' over the North Curve to Rhondda Cutting Junction. It was during such a manoeuvre, on 19th October, 1878, that the empty Llantrisant branch train was reversed into the path of a down Rhondda branch passenger train, killing 12 passengers and injuring a further 103. Although direct responsibility was placed on the signalman at Northern Junction, Colonel Yolland, the Board of Trade Inspector, was also highly critical of the practice of working 'wrong line' over the North Curve, together with the generally inadequate signalling arrangements at the junctions themselves. In response to Yolland's concerns, a trailing crossover and full interlocking were installed at Northern Junction.

This accident gave renewed impetus to the installation, throughout the TVR, of modern signalling arrangements. This had commenced in 1876, following earlier recommendations from the Board of Trade, but in 1878 the L&TVJR was still signalled on the outdated 'station signal' principle, with a double-armed home signal centrally positioned at stations or sidings, protected by distant signals in both directions. Full protection could not be provided under such a system, and considerable reliance was placed on the train crew's knowledge of the road.

The rather sparse passenger train service on the L&TVJR was augmented in

July 1879, with the introduction of an additional return working in the mid afternoon. This established the basic pattern of service which was to continue throughout the 1880s. Two minor incidents involving branch trains during this period are of interest. On 29th January, 1880 an axle broke on the brake van of a down mineral train, blocking the single line, just above Common Branch Junction. As the 6.40 pm ex-Llantrisant was unable to pass this obstruction, its passengers (about 30) were detrained and taken forward to Pontypridd in an open goods wagon. On 15th April, 1882 the leading wheels of the first down passenger train of the day were forced off the line, near Cross Inn, as a result of a piece of iron having been placed on the track. Luckily, the train was travelling slowly at the time, so there were no injuries.

Passenger traffic was at a relatively low level at this time, as shown by figures for the six months ending 31st December, 1886:

Tickets issued to and from Llantrisant Branch stations

	Single Tickets	Return Tickets	Total*
Llantwit	9,391	1,353	12,097
Cross Inn	11,000	2,955	16,910
Llantrisant TVR	18,949	2,015	22,979

* Includes 2 trips for each return ticket

This represented a daily average of 333 trips, or about 40 per train. Even with this low level of usage, however, there was still pressure for improved services. By the late 1880s development in the Llantwit Fardre district had produced a settlement pattern which was not fully served by stations on the L&TVJR. On 24th March, 1887 a deputation from a committee representing residents of Llantwit Fardre, Llantrisant and Cowbridge attended the TVR Board to press for an improved train service and a new station at Church Village, about a mile east of Llantwit station. Any increase in frequency, however, was ruled out on the grounds that there was inadequate capacity on the single line branch, together with insufficient traffic to justify the running of additional trains.

The request for a station at Church Village was received more favourably, however, and on 28th April, 1887 instructions were given for it to be provided. Church Village station was built by Mr Mathias of Porth, and opened on 1st October, 1887, an occasion for great rejoicing in the neighbourhood.

Having peaked in the early 1870s, iron ore production at the Bute and Mwyndy mines went into decline, leading to a significant loss of traffic for the L&TVJR. The Bute mine closed in 1880, followed by Mwyndy in 1884, leaving Trecastle as the last producer in the area. The Bute mine had been taken over by the Dowlais Iron Co. in 1873, but a year earlier the Dowlais Company, in conjunction with the Consett Iron Co. of Durham and Krupps of Essen, had formed the Orconera Co. to develop Spanish sources of iron ore. Importation of Spanish ore was to sound the death knell of the local haematite mines, and in 1891 Trecastle finally succumbed to foreign competition, ending the transport of iron ore over the L&TVJR, at least until the opening of the Llanharry mine in the present century.

Fortunately, the early 1880s also saw something of a resurgence in the local coal industry. In February 1884 the *South Wales Daily News* reported that the area was 'reviving from its long state of dormancy'. The Garth Llantwit Colliery Co. was reopening the old Ystradbarwig pit. Also reopening were Llest Llantwit and Gelynog pits. Ystradbarwig was re-connected to the L&TVJR in 1883 but proved extremely short-lived, the siding being reported out of use in 1885. The most significant development came with the completion of a rail link, in the form of the Treferig Valley Railway, to Glyn Colliery, near Tonyrefail, in 1883 (*see Chapter 6*).

The passenger and goods facilities at Llantrisant station had gradually been added to since its opening as a small wayside station on the SWR in 1850. By the late 1880s however, they had become grossly inadequate for the needs of the traffic. TVR trains, in particular, were confined to the very restricted bay platform on the down side of the station. When changes were proposed, however, they did not get a warm welcome from the TVR. On 12th May, 1887 the TVR Traffic Manager, James Hurman, informed his Directors that the GWR had put forward proposals for improving arrangements at Llantrisant, but that this was likely to involve the TVR in considerable expense. In addition to demanding that the TVR share in the costs of the improvements, the GWR also wished to take over station work undertaken by the TVR, as provided for under the agreement between the GWR and the Cowbridge Railway of 9th January, 1864. The TVR responded by preparing plans for an independent line from the L&TVJR, just above Maesaraul Junction, to join the Cowbridge line and avoiding Llantrisant station. When negotiations failed to produce a mutually acceptable outcome, the TVR deposited plans for this railway, as part of its Additional Powers Bill for the 1888 Session. Confrontation was avoided, however, when this proposal was withdrawn as part of an agreement, dated 14th March, 1888, between the two companies. Under the terms of this agreement, the GWR undertook to carry out improvements at Llantrisant station, with the TVR paying interest at seven per cent per annum on its contribution (put at £900) to the total cost of the alterations. The rebuilt station provided far better facilities for the TVR, with an extended run-round loop in the Cowbridge bay and improved passenger accommodation on the down platform, being completed in 1891.

The building of the main line and Treforest branch (both opened on 18th July, 1889) of the Barry Dock and Railway brought with it radical changes to local railway geography in the vicinity of Tonteg. The new railway took a higher level route along the western side of the Taff Vale, being joined at Tonteg by the branch from Treforest, which had climbed from its junction with the TVR, at a gradient of 1 in 101. Shortly after leaving Tonteg Junction, the Barry main line passed under a girder bridge carrying the L&TVJR.

Over the years the TVR had accumulated, on lease, a number of nominally independent companies, the most extensive of which was the L&TVJR. On 26th August, 1889 an Act was obtained which brought most of these concerns within the TVR fold. The TVR (Amalgamations and Capital) Act authorised the absorption of the L&TVJR by the TVR, although the actual amalgamation was effective from 1st July, 1889. With the passing of this Act the last vestiges of the L&TVJR's independent existence faded away.

ANNO VICESIMO NONO & TRICESIMO

VICTORIÆ REGINÆ.

****

Cap. ccxlviii.

An Act to enable the *Llantrissant and Taff Vale
Junction* Railway Company to make Railways to
join the Railway of the *Penarth* Harbour, Dock,
and Railway Company, and the *Ely Valley* Railway, and to form an additional Junction with
their *Llantrissant Common* Branch ; and for other
Purposes.   */23ᵈ July 1866/*

W HEREAS by "The *Llantrissant and Taff Vale Junction*   24 & 25 Vict.
Railway Act, 1861," the *Llantrissant and Taff Vale*   c. li.
Junction Railway Company (herein called "the Com-
pany") were incorporated, and authorized to make a Railway com-
mencing by a Junction with the *Taff Vale* Railway in the Parish of
Llantwit Vardre, and terminating in the Parish of *Llantrissant*, with
Two Branches therefrom, called respectively in the said Act "the
Ely Junction Branch" and "the *Llantrissant Common* Branch:"
And whereas it is expedient that the Company should be authorized
to make and maintain Railways for the Purpose of connecting their
Railway with the Railway of the *Penarth* Harbour, Dock, and Railway
Company, and with the *Ely Valley* Railway, and also a Railway to
afford

Title page for the Llantrissant and Taff Vale Junction Railway Act, 1866.

Chapter Five

The L&TVJR New Lines
1865-1889

At the time of its inception in 1860 the main object of the L&TVJR was the transport of Mwyndy iron ore to the iron works at Merthyr and the heads of the valleys, with coal traffic very much a secondary consideration. By 1865, however, the focus of attention had shifted westwards to the rapidly developing coalfield of the Ogmore valley. After years of indecision, delay and frustration, the TVR eventually obtained its own route to the Ogmore valley, only to be denied a worthwhile traffic, as a result of other developments in the local railway network which had taken place in the intervening period.

In the early 1860s the firm of John Brogden and Son had leased extensive mineral property in the Ogmore valley from the Duchy of Lancaster. In order to provide an outlet for their coal, the Brogdens promoted the Ogmore Valley Railways (OVR). This was incorporated by Act of 13th July, 1863 to build a standard gauge line from Nantymoel, at the head of the Ogmore valley, to a junction with the Llynvi Valley Railway (LVR) at Tondu. The Act also empowered the OVR to lay a third rail over the broad gauge LVR from Tondu to Porthcawl, from where coal could be shipped at the tidal dock. The OVR, together with this mixed gauge section, opened to mineral traffic on 1st August, 1865, the third rail being laid over the whole of the LVR by 1868.

Also incorporated in 1863 was the Ely Valley Extension Railway (EVER), forming a continuation of the Gellyrhaidd branch of the EVR into the valley of the Ogmore Fach. The Brogdens acquired shares in the new company, so that when the contractor, Mr Lumley, failed to complete the line within the terms of his contract, they were able to step in and take over the unfinished works. Instructions were given to lay a third rail over the new railway, and in this form the EVER was opened to mineral traffic on 16th October, 1865. As its only outlet was via the broad gauge EVR, however, the EVER could only be worked by broad gauge trains provided by the GWR until the gauge conversion of 1872. The EVER remained isolated from the rest of the Brogden empire until the opening of the Blackmill-Hendreforgan line in 1875.

The decision to employ the standard gauge meant that the OVR, surrounded as it was by broad gauge lines, lacked an effective outlet for its traffic. Porthcawl could offer only its old tidal dock, whilst access to Cardiff was hampered by the need for transhipment at Stormy, near Pyle, and the very limited accommodation for the broad gauge at the docks themselves. The Brogdens' first move was to promote the construction of a new dock at Porthcawl. For this they joined forces with the LVR to obtain the Llynvi and Ogmore Railways Act of 23rd June, 1864. This authorised the construction of a new dock at the northern end of the old basin at Porthcawl, and also provided for the formation of a joint committee to own and manage the harbour. The dock was engineered by Mr R.P. Brereton at a cost of £250,000, and opened on 22nd July, 1867.

In spite of this substantial investment, Porthcawl was never to provide a

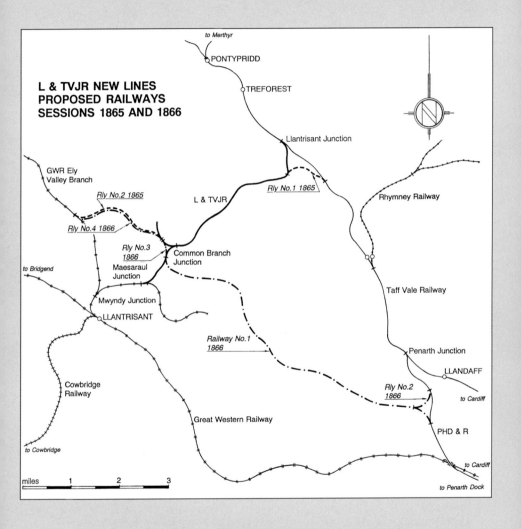

L & TVJR NEW LINES
PROPOSED RAILWAYS
SESSIONS 1865 AND 1866

to Merthyr

PONTYPRIDD

TREFOREST

Llantrisant Junction

Rly No.1 1865

GWR Ely
Valley Branch

Rly No.2 1865

L & TVJR

Rhymney Railway

Rly No.4 1866

*Rly No.3
1866*

Common Branch
Junction

Maesaraul
Junction

to Bridgend

Taff Vale Railway

Mwyndy Junction

LLANTRISANT

*Railway No.1
1866*

Penarth Junction

LLANDAFF

*Rly No.2
1866*

to Cardiff

Cowbridge
Railway

Great Western Railway

PHD & R

to Cowbridge

to Cardiff

miles   1   2   3

to Penarth Dock

really effective answer to the OVR's problems. This was partly due to the inherent difficulties caused by the presence of Tusker Rock, near the approach to the harbour, and partly because the main market for bituminous coal was the ironworks at the heads of the valleys.

The Brogdens seem to have been well aware of these shortcomings, even before the new dock opened. Indeed, as early as October 1863 Henry Voss, GWR Engineer with responsibility for the EVR, informed the GWR Chairman, Sir Daniel Gooch, that the Brogdens had asked for a third rail to be laid over the EVR. If this was not done, the Brogdens threatened to seek an arrangement with the L&TVJR and TVR, with a third rail over the intervening section of the EVR. No action was forthcoming, however, and in August 1864 Alex Brogden pressed the GWR to lay a third rail over its South Wales main line, between Bridgend and Cardiff. The response was non-committal and in November 1864 the Brogdens deposited two sets of plans for railways from the OVR at Blackmill, to join the L&TVJR, and the PHD&R and TVR near Llandaff. The two proposals were broadly similar, except that the New Works No. 1 Bill included a section parallel to the EVR between Hendreforgan and Ynysmaerdy, whereas the New Works No. 2 Bill envisaged running powers over this section.

This scheme represented a significant incursion into territory only recently annexed by the L&TVJR, on behalf of the TVR. At the same time, the traffic potential of the Ogmore valley was attracting the attention of the TVR. On 6th October, 1864 the company's Engineer and General Superintendent, George Fisher, had reported at length on this subject. He had investigated various ways of tapping the Ogmore traffic, including tunnelling through from the Rhondda Fawr branch, but had concluded that a southerly route was the best option. Following on from this, plans were deposited by the L&TVJR in November 1864, for a south curve at Maesmawr and an extension of the Common branch to join the EVR, near Ynysmaerdy. Plans were also deposited by Richard Bassett of the EVR and Henry Voss for the Ely and Ogmore Valleys Junction Railway, from the EVR at Hendreforgan to a triangular junction with the OVR at Blackmill.

Little came of all this activity, however: the OVR Bills were thrown out on Standing Orders, and the E&OVJR and L&TVJR Bills were rejected early in their passage through the House.

By October 1865 the dust had settled after the struggle of the previous Session and it was clear that little had changed. In particular, the OVR remained isolated from the standard gauge network. To overcome this problem the Brogdens proposed that the L&TVJR construct an extension of the Common branch to join the OVR at Blackmill, bypassing the EVR. In return, they offered to abandon their attempt to reach the PHD&R, via an independent route, and to provide half the capital needed for the Common branch - Blackmill link. As such a scheme would have represented a direct assault on GWR territory, the TVR was reluctant to risk a confrontation. As a result, the suggested joint venture was not pursued, and the Brogdens were forced to take up the fight again in the 1866 Session. In November 1865 the OVR deposited plans for new railways between Blackmill and Cardiff and Penarth. Two Bills were involved: New Works (No. 1) and New Works (No. 2). New Works (No. 1) provided the link between Blackmill and the Common branch, while New Works (No. 2) formed a continuation to join the PHD&R, the TVR, and the authorised Cardiff and Caerphilly Railway of the Rhymney Railway Company (RR).

The TVR's response took the form of a new line from the L&TVJR at Common Branch Junction to the PHD&R (Railway No. 1), together with an extension of the Common branch to joint the EVR at Ynysmaerdy. A west curve at Common Branch Junction was also proposed.

The GWR also entered the fray, both in its own right and also under the guise of its satellite, the EVR. In its Further Powers Bill, the GWR proposed a northern curve at Mwyndy Junction on the EVR, three short connecting lines between the South Wales main line and the PHD&R, and an extension of the EVR to Blaenclydach, overlooking the Rhondda Fawr valley. The Bill also included powers for altering the gauge of the EVR and the GWR generally. The EVR's contribution took the form of an extension of the Common branch, along similar lines to that proposed in the L&TVJR Bill, and a Hendreforgan - Blackmill link. Plans were also deposited by colliery owners David Davies ('Davies the Ocean') and Ebenezer Lewis for the Ely Valley and Vale of Neath Junction Railway from Penrhiwfer to the head of the Rhondda Fawr, at Blaenrhondda. Taken together, these various lines would have enabled coal from the Rhondda Fawr, Ely and Ogmore valleys to pass directly to Cardiff, Penarth and possibly Barry, had the original Barry Railway, incorporated in 1865, been built.

Pressure for the introduction of the standard gauge over GWR lines in South Wales, either by conversion or the addition of a third rail, reached a peak in early 1866. On 2nd March, 1866 the half-yearly meeting of the company's shareholders was informed that a memorial had been received, signed by nearly every firm of any standing in South Wales, requesting the provision of the standard gauge. In August 1866 the GWR Directors announced that they intended to proceed with conversion of the EVR and the mixing of the gauge between Llantrisant and Newport, as soon as resources would permit. This intention was soon overtaken by the financial crisis of 1866, however, and in March 1867 the GWR Directors reported, with regret, that they had been unable to proceed with this project because of the 'continuance of the monetary pressure as affecting railways, and the necessity of confining the expenditure of the Company within the strictest limits.' *Plus ca change!*

The TVR and GWR joined forces to counter the OVR New Works Bills in the 1866 Session, arguing that the lines proposed were largely unnecessary. This contention found favour with Parliament, and the Brogdens' scheme was rejected, with the exception of the section between Hendreforgan and Blackmill, which was authorised by the OVR Act of 23rd July, 1866. The L&TVJR New Lines Bill was accepted in its entirety, also receiving Royal Assent on 23rd July, 1866. The EVR Bill was withdrawn, the GWR representative having given a verbal assurance in Committee that his company would lay the third rail over the EVR between Ynysmaerdy and Hendreforgan. The GWR proposals were also authorised, with the exception of the extension of the Ely Valley line north of Penygraig, which was eventually provided for by the Ely and Clydach Valleys Railway Act 1873.

Work on the New Lines got off to a reasonably quick start. In November 1866 it was reported that Railway No. 1 was being pegged out. The following February the L&TVJR Directors were able to report the completion of surveys for the extension of the Common Branch to join the EVR, and that they would shortly be ready to invite tenders for its construction. This momentum was maintained in May 1867, when orders were given to start work on the west curve at Common Branch Junction (Railway No. 3). By this time, however, the consequences of the financial crisis of the previous year were becoming only too clear. At the half-yearly meeting of L&TVJR shareholders on 27th August, 1867 the Board announced that, although surveys and contract drawings had been completed and the contract let for Railway No. 3, they had refrained from proceeding with other parts of the New Lines project because of the depressed state of trade.

It was not until 1869 that activity was resumed. In May of that year the TVR was warned that the time limit for taking possession of lands expired on 23rd July, 1869. Having made an inspection of the district, the TVR Board gave instructions, at its meeting on 25th June, 1869, for plans to be brought forward for the Common branch extension (Railway No. 4). At the next meeting, on 30th July, 1869, George Fisher was requested to report on the question of an application to Parliament for an extension of time for the completion of Railway No. 1, and the abandonment of Railway No. 2 (the northern curve at Waterhall Junction). Also, at this meeting, the tender of Mr Billups, of Cardiff, was accepted for the construction of Railway No. 4.

By the middle of 1870 Railway No. 3 was complete, and work was under way on Railway No. 4, but little progress had been made with the major element of the New Lines scheme, Railway No. 1. An extension of time was obtained under the L&TVJR Act of 20th June, 1870, together with the abandonment of Railway No. 2. In addition, the TVR undertook to convey traffic from the L&TVJR lines and connections, via Llantrisant Junction, to Cardiff and Penarth, at the rates it would have charged had the direct route via Railway No. 1 been available.

The lack of progress with Railway No. 1 was echoed by that on the authorised OVR line between Blackmill and Hendreforgan. In 1866 the OVR had been amalgamated with the Llynvi Valley Railway to form the Llynvi and Ogmore Railway (L&OR), with an extension of time for the completion of the Blackmill-Hendreforgan line being obtained in 1869. By the middle of 1870, however, little had been done, apart from the foundations and walls of a bridge at Blackmill. Meanwhile, the GWR had still not laid the third rail over the EVR. This lack of activity was in marked contrast to the progress being made with the exploitation of the coal measures of the Ogmore valley. The bituminous reserves were being extensively worked, while the steam coal had been proved, and was in the process of being developed, particularly by David Davies and Company.

On 30th August, 1870 George Fisher reported this general lack of progress to his Directors. He had become convinced that the L&OR had no intention of constructing the Blackmill-Hendreforgan line as a link between its system and the TVR. His suspicions had been aroused by the presence, in the area, of LNWR surveyors, with instructions to draw up plans for a route from L&OR to the Rhymney Railway, north of Walnut Tree Junction. Although somewhat circuitous for traffic destined for Cardiff and Penarth, such a route was well-suited as a link between the L&OR and the inland markets for bituminous coal. It would then have seriously undermined the value of the L&TVJR New Lines. In response, George Fisher recommended that the GWR should be pressed to lay the long-promised third rail on the EVR, and that plans should be prepared for an independent line between the L&TVJR and Blackmill. On 30th September, 1870 Fisher was instructed to prepare a survey of the district between the Ogmore and Ely valleys.

George Fisher's fears were soon shown to be well-founded. In November 1870 plans were deposited by the L&OR for a grandiose scheme linking Blackmill to the RR. The proposed line would have been heavily engineered, with two lengthy tunnels, one of 210 yards near Treferig, and the other of 447 yards just before the line crossed the Taff valley, which was to be achieved by means of an 18-arch viaduct, 400 yards long, with a maximum height of 123 feet. Significantly, powers were sought to enable the LNWR and the RR to subscribe towards the capital of the undertaking, and to enter into working and traffic agreements with the L&OR. Whilst for the L&OR the line provided a route to inland markets, for the LNWR it offered a means of access into the very heart of the GWR's South Wales empire, a tempting prize indeed.

In response, the TVR deposited plans for the Ely and Ogmore Valleys Junction Railways, involving a new line from Hendreforgan to a triangular junction with the L&OR, at Blackmill. In the event of this proving unacceptable to Parliament, powers were also sought to compel the L&OR to complete its authorised line between Blackmill and Hendreforgan.

For the GWR the threat posed by the L&OR Bill was clearly of major strategic importance, especially given the involvement of the LNWR. It exposed the underlying vulnerability of the company in the face of continuing pressure to abandon the broad gauge in South Wales. Faced with such a threat, the issue of gauge conversion could be deferred no longer. On 24th November, 1870, at a meeting with representatives of the TVR, GWR officers announced their company's decision to convert the Ely Valley and South Wales lines to standard gauge. This was accompanied by a suggestion that the two companies should agree to a division of traffic receipts on traffic passing from Ogmore valley to Cardiff and Penarth.

The decision to abandon the broad gauge soon had its desired effect. The L&OR Bill was withdrawn, as was the E&OVJR Bill, on the understanding that tripartite discussions would take place with a view to reaching an agreement covering the provision, by the GWR, of the standard gauge between Hendreforgan and Llantrisant Common Junction, and the completion of the Blackmill-Hendreforgan line by the L&OR. These works were to be completed by 1st September, 1871, with the TVR being granted running powers between Llantrisant Common Junction and Hendreforgan. Several meetings took place, but negotiations reached an impasse when the L&OR tried to introduce additional clauses which the TVR felt were out of keeping with the original understanding.

The most important consequence of the 1870 confrontation, however, was the ending of the broad gauge in South Wales in May 1872. Up until then, the break of gauge had prevented a connection being made between the L&TVJR's Common branch extension and the EVR, at Llantrisant Common Junction. Unfortunately, the GWR refused to permit this connection to be made on the grounds that powers for making the junction, contained in the L&TVJR Act 1866, had been allowed to lapse. Faced with continuing GWR intransigence on this point, the TVR was forced to seek fresh powers in the 1873 Session. It also took the opportunity to apply for running powers over the EVR, EVER and Ogmore valley lines, north of Llantrisant Common Junction.

This Bill was petitioned against by the GWR and the L&OR, but on 25th March, 1873 an agreement was entered into whereby the petitions were withdrawn in return for the deletion of the application for running powers. Under this agreement, the junction itself was to be constructed, but as there was insufficient land nearby on which to lay interchange sidings, these were to be provided, at the joint and equal expense of the three companies, at the junction between EVR and the EVER at Gellyrhaidd, or at some other suitable point between there and Llantrisant Common Junction. If these sidings were constructed, the L&TVJR was to have running powers over the intervening section of the EVR in respect of traffic from the Ogmore valley destined for the TVR system. This agreement was confirmed by the L&TVJR Act of 21st July, 1873, which also extended the time limit for the completion of Railway No. 1 of the company's 1866 Act for a further 3 years, to 20th June, 1877. Although the interchange sidings were never constructed, another feature of the 1873 agreement was later to be of benefit to the TVR. This provided for the agreement of through routes and facilities for goods and mineral traffic from the Ogmore valleys, destined for Cardiff, Penarth and other places on the TVR.

On 2nd June, 1874 the L&TVJR Board was informed that Llantrisant Common Junction had been completed. Delay in agreeing traffic arrangements with the GWR prevented its opening, however, and it was not until 21st January, 1875 that George Fisher was able to announce that it was expected to open on 25th February, 1875.

The gauge conversion of 1872 opened up a new, if somewhat indirect, route from the Ogmore valley to Cardiff, via Bridgend. Meanwhile, the Blackmill-Hendreforgan link remained in limbo. Although the tender of Mr Hanson for its construction had been accepted on 25th January, 1871, progress was very slow, the scheme being kept alive by an extension of time under the L&OR Act of 21st July, 1873.

This lack of progress was in stark contrast to that of another scheme which had emerged to connect the Ogmore valley to Cardiff and Penarth. In November 1872 David Davies, no doubt dissatisfied with the existing route via Bridgend, deposited plans for the Cardiff and Ogmore Railway (C&OR), to run from Nantymoel, at the head of the Ogmore valley, to Llanharran, on the South Wales main line, with a short connection to the L&OR, just north of Blackmill. At the same time the L&OR deposited a Bill for a line from Tondu to Pencoed, also on the South Wales main line. Both proposals were sanctioned by Parliament, receiving Royal Assent on 21st July, 1873, with the exception of the section of the C&OR to the north of Blackmill. However, the Acts contained

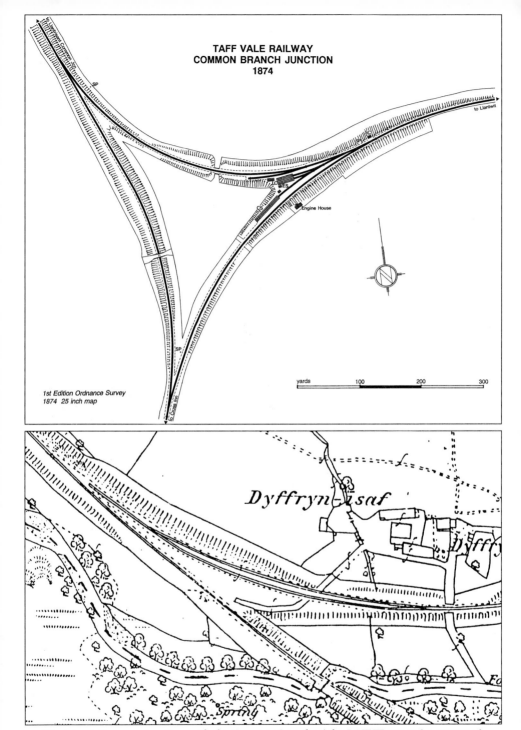

**TAFF VALE RAILWAY
COMMON BRANCH JUNCTION
1874**

SP

to Llantrisant Common Br..

to Llantwit

to Cross Inn

LC..
ES

Engine House

SP

to Cross Inn

yards 100 200 300

1st Edition Ordnance Survey
1874 25 inch map

Dyffryn-isaf

Dyff

Spring

Fo..

Llantrisant Common Junction, with the Common branch of the L&TVJR yet to be connected
with the Ely Valley line. *Reproduced from the 25″, 1874 Ordnance Survey Map*

clauses designed to avoid duplication of facilities, by enabling one line only to be built from what was to become Bryncethin Junction, where the two lines were to pass close to each other, to either Pencoed or Llanharran. The network that eventually emerged was, therefore, a compromise between the two schemes, with the C&OR being built from Blackmill to Llanharran (opened 2nd October, 1876) and the L&OR line from Tondu to Bryncethin Junction (opened 1st May, 1877). Meanwhile the C&OR had been amalgamated with the L&OR by Act of 24th July, 1876. Work had also been progressing, with increased vigour, on the Hendreforgan-Blackmill line, which was opened on 1st September, 1875.

Following their 1870 confrontation, the GWR took an increasing interest in the affairs of the L&OR, leading to the establishment of a working agreement between the two companies on 16th May, 1873, followed by full amalgamation under the GWR Act of 1st July, 1883.

The opening of the C&OR provided a direct route for coal traffic from the Ogmore valley to Cardiff and Penarth, the latter being via the Penarth Curves, authorised by the GWR (Further Powers) Act 1866 and reported to be complete and ready for Board of Trade inspection in April 1876. As a result, even with the completion of the Hendreforgan-Blackmill line in 1875, the need for L&TVJR Railway No. 1 was greatly diminished. With its powers for construction due to expire on 20th June, 1877, the case for abandonment had become very strong indeed. From the TVR's point of view, however, it was essential that this question should be linked to that of the apportionment of receipts from traffic from the Ogmore valley to Cardiff and Penarth. Abandonment was not a straightforward option, however, as the L&TVJR Act of 1866 contained an onerous penalty clause, entitling landowners to substantial compensation in the event of non-completion of Railway No. 1. About ¼ mile of earthworks and a substantial bridge had been constructed at the Common Branch Junction end of the railway, leaving about 6¾ miles to complete. Matters were further complicated by the fact that a small colliery had been opened at Tynycoed, near Creigiau, on the route of Railway No. 1. It was feared that the owner, Moses Rowlands, might seek compensation on the grounds that he had opened his colliery in the reasonable expectation of the railway being built. So concerned was the TVR over this possibility, that serious consideration was given to building only that section of Railway No. 1 from Common Branch Junction to Tynycoed Colliery, with the rest of the line being abandoned.

After further consideration, and having taken legal advice, it was determined that the best course of action was to seek an extension of time in the 1877 Session, followed by a Bill of abandonment the following year. Accordingly, a Bill was deposited for a further extension of time for Railway No. 1.

Meanwhile, negotiations continued on the linked issue of the apportionment of receipts from Ogmore valley traffic. Progress was marred, however, when the GWR promoted the Ely and Rhondda Valley Junction Railway Bill in the 1877 Session. This proposal involved an extension from the EVR at Penrhiwfer into and up the Rhondda Fawr valley, in direct competition to the TVR. This line was intended to counter the TVR's Bill of the same session for a railway from its Rhondda Fawr branch to the EVR, near Penygraig. Sanity prevailed, however, and agreement was reached to withdraw both schemes, leaving only the L&TVJR extension of time Bill to pass through Parliament. A further source of dispute arose when the GWR petitioned against this Bill on the mistaken assumption that this would assist with the subsequent abandonment of Railway No. 1. This petition was withdrawn following a forceful intervention from George Fisher, who argued that it could in fact prejudice the aim of eventual abandonment of Railway No. 1. On 2nd August, 1877 Royal Assent was obtained for a further extension of time for Railway No. 1, to 20th June, 1880.

The abandonment Bill was not proceeded with, however, because of continuing failure to reach agreement on the apportionment of the Ogmore valleys receipts. In order to keep Railway No. 1 alive, and thereby avoid any claims for compensation, a fourth extension of time was sought in the 1880 Session. This was in spite of GWR requests to proceed with abandonment, but was done without any great enthusiasm on the part of the TVR Directors, for whom Railway No. 1 had become an unnecessary and embarrassing relic of earlier ambitions and different circumstances.

All this changed, however, on 8th May, 1880, when the TVR Board resolved to complete Railway No. 1, if the extension of time Bill, then before Parliament, proved successful. The motive behind this dramatic change of heart was the prospect of coal traffic from the area served by the proposed Treferig Valley Railway, which had been incorporated by Act of 21st July, 1879, coupled with the threat of GWR competition for this traffic (*see Chapter 6*). With a new sense of commitment behind it, the Act providing for a fourth extension of time for Railway No. 1 received Royal Assent on 29th June, 1880.

It was soon apparent that this renewal of powers was not to be the hollow formality of earlier Acts. As a short section of Railway No. 1 had been built at the Common Branch Junction end in the 1860s, it was possible to make a fairly rapid start on the works. On 30th October, 1880 application was made for Board of Trade sanction for a new connection with Railway No. 1, at Common Branch Junction. By this date, Railway No. 3, authorised by the L&TVJR Act 1866 - the west curve at Common Branch Junction - had been lifted; indeed it is doubtful if any use was ever made of this line. The new junction to Railway No. 1 comprised a single turnout in the single track main line, fully signalled and controlled by a new signal box, known as Common Branch Junction West. Provisional sanction was granted by the Board of Trade on 1st November, 1880, enabling the new works to be brought into use prior to inspection. This was reported on on 30th November, 1880, by Colonel Rich for the Board of Trade. Colonel Rich noted that it was not intended that the new signal box should be manned at all times, and that the up and down signals would be locked when the box was not in use. He was satisfied that the arrangements complied with Board of Trade requirements, and recommended that full sanction should be granted for the use of the new junction.

Progress with Railway No. 1 was not rapid, however and by 12th January, 1882, when George Fisher reported the position to the TVR Board, little had been achieved. Notice to treat had been served on all landowners, although, in several cases, prices had still not been agreed. In these circumstances, Fisher sought instructions as to whether or not the Board wished to continue work on

Railway No. 1.

Work continued, nevertheless, perhaps with added stimulus provided by the incorporation of the Barry Dock and Railway Company (BD&R) on 14th August, 1884, after an unsuccessful attempt in the previous Session. The main line of the BD&R from Cadoxton to Trehavod was to pass close to the L&TVJR's Railway No. 1 at Creigiau, and both the 1883 and 1884 Barry schemes envisaged a connection between the two railways at this point. Such a link would have enabled the Barry Company to abstract traffic from the L&TVJR and Treferig, Ely and Ogmore valleys, via Railway No. 1. In the event, the Creigiau junction line was not constructed, although a temporary connection was put in at Creigiau to enable BD&R contractors, Messrs Lovat and Shaw, to bring in materials for the new works by rail. On 13th September, 1886, TVR Traffic Manager, James Hurman, was informed that this connection was ready for traffic. It was removed following the cessation of construction traffic.

Meanwhile, application for Board of Trade sanction for the connection between Railway No. 1 and the PHD&R at Waterhall Junction had been submitted on 29th May, 1886. It was inspected by Colonel Rich, who completed his report on 5th June, 1886. The layout was unusual in that it comprised a trailing connection only from Railway No. 1 to the down line of the PHD&R, with a single slip in the crossing of the up line, thereby providing a trailing crossover between up and down Penarth lines. From the outset trains were always propelled over Railway No. 1 from Waterhall Junction to Common Branch Junction. In the opposite direction, trains from Railway No. 1, bound for Radyr, were reversed over the crossover, before being propelled over the up Penarth line to their destination. Railway No. 1 was opened to goods and mineral traffic only on 11th September, 1886.

The opening of the Llantrisant No. 1 Railway (as Railway No. 1 was henceforth known) completed the basic network of the New Lines authorised by the L&TVJR Act 1866. By 1886, however, the original objective had long since been overtaken by developments elsewhere, such as the gauge conversion in South Wales and the building of the C&OR. Only very limited traffic was ever attracted to the New Lines and what there was was derived from sources served by the L&TVJR itself and from the Treferig Valley Railway, rather than from the Ogmore and Ely valleys. Speaking about Llantrisant No. 1 Railway in 1910, Ammon Beasley, the TVR General Manager, said 'There is very little traffic on it and it need never have been constructed'. Nevertheless, some financial benefit did accrue to the TVR in return for the not inconsiderable resources it had invested in its ill-fated Ogmore valley adventure. It will be recalled that, under agreement between the GWR, L&OR and TVR of 25th March, 1873, provision had been made for through rates and facilities for goods and mineral traffic from the Ogmore valleys to Cardiff, Penarth and other places on the TVR. In January 1885, fearing that the completion of Railway No. 1 would result in the diversion of traffic from its own lines, the GWR suggested a new basis for the apportionment of receipts from traffic from the Llynfi and Ogmore valleys to Cardiff and Penarth. On 23rd June, 1887 James Hurman, TVR Traffic Manager, was able to inform his Board that agreement had finally been reached with the GWR on this subject.

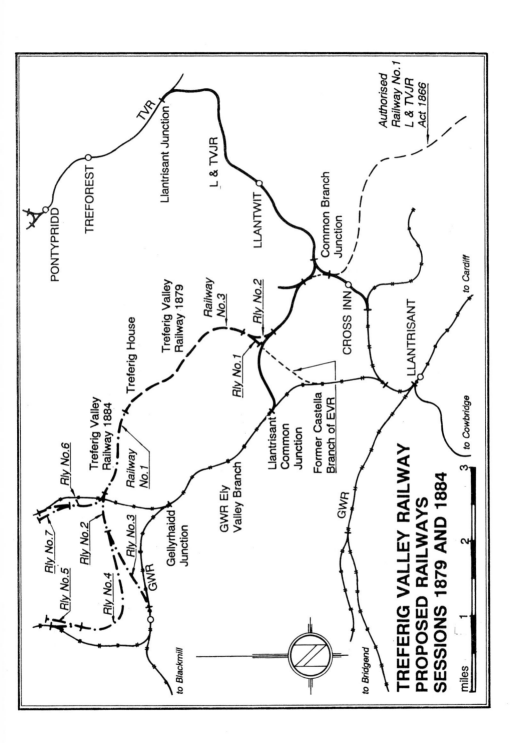

TREFERIG VALLEY RAILWAY
PROPOSED RAILWAYS
SESSIONS 1879 AND 1884

Chapter Six

The Treferig Valley Railway
1879-1889

The narrow wooded valley of the Nant Mychydd (otherwise known as the Treferig valley), to the north of Llantrisant, has the appearance of having escaped the ravages of the coal industry in the 19th century. Closer examination, however, will reveal the course of a long disused railway, now in an advanced state of reabsorption into the landscape, together with faint traces of former mining activity at the head of the valley. These relics are all that remain of largely unfulfilled ambitions for exploiting the mineral resources of the valley.

Penetration of the Treferig valley featured in a number of early schemes, starting with Overton's tramroad branch of 1823. These proposals all followed a broadly similar course from the Taff Vale, at or near Maesmawr, via Cross Inn and Llantrisant Common. The first railway to enter the Treferig valley, however, was the Glanmychydd or Castellau branch of the EVR, which followed the natural route provided by the Nant Mychydd from the Ely valley. Unfortunately, little traffic was attracted to this branch and on 29th December, 1866, Henry Voss, GWR Engineer with responsibility for the EVR, advised his Directors to take up the rails for use elsewhere. This recommendation was accepted on 31st January, 1867, the rails being lifted shortly afterwards. It is clear, however, that it was envisaged that the rails would, in due course, be reinstated, but this was not to be the case, and the Castellau branch remained disused, although it was not formally abandoned until 1926.

Later schemes sought to make use of the valley as an independent route between the L&TVJR and the Ely and Ogmore valleys, rather than as a worthwhile destination in its own right. Its traffic potential was limited by difficult geological conditions: the presence of the Pontypridd Anticline and Llantwit-Caerphilly Syncline meant that steam and bituminous coal measures were readily accessible in the upper reaches of the valley. Further down the valley, however, the depth of the steam coal measures increased beyond reach, leaving only house coal reserves accessible, although somewhat fragmented. Until the 1870s only very limited mining had taken place in the lower reaches of the valley. The first, and as events were to prove, only successful attempt to exploit the steam coal measures of the upper part of the valley, came with the sinking, by the mid 1870s, of Glyn Colliery, near Tonyrefail. Lacking rail access, however, the potential of this colliery was decidedly limited.

This deficiency was keenly felt by a number of lessees of mineral rights in the valley, and in November 1878 they deposited a Bill for the Treferig Valley Railway. This was to follow a lightly engineered and somewhat sinuous route from a junction with the Common branch of the L&TVJR to Glyn Colliery (Railways Nos. 2 and 3). In addition, a short branch (Railway No. 1) was to run from this 'main line' to an end-on junction with the defunct Castellau branch of the EVR. The promoters also sought powers to enter into working and traffic agreements with both the GWR and the TVR.

Reporting this development to the TVR Board on 12th December, 1878, George Fisher predicted that the Treferig promoters could be expected to offer their line to either the GWR or the TVR, and warned that in the event of one company taking up the offer, the other could be denied access to the valley. Thus, construction of Railways Nos. 2 and 3 would secure the Treferig valley for the TVR, whilst completion of Railways Nos. 1 and 3, together with the reopening of the Castellau branch, would ensure a GWR monopoly. In the light of this, the TVR opposed the Treferig Valley Railway Bill in Parliament. Further conflict was averted, however, in February 1879, when the Treferig promoters agreed to the insertion of a clause undertaking to open all three railways simultaneously and not to give any differential rate or advantage to either company. On this basis, the TVR opposition was withdrawn and the Treferig Valley Railway Act received Royal Assent on 21st July, 1879.

As incorporated in 1879 the Treferig Company had its capital set at £15,000, with borrowing powers for a further £5,000. Five years were allowed for completion of the railways and the company was authorised to enter into working and traffic agreements with the TVR and the GWR.

Little progress was made, however, as the promoters were unable to raise sufficient finance to construct their railway. On 21st February, 1880 Treferig Chairman, Mr Tudor Crawshay, approached the TVR Board with a request for assistance. In response, the Board instructed George Fisher to investigate the traffic potential of the Treferig Valley Railway. He was also instructed, on 8th March, 1880, to seek the views of the GWR on the Treferig scheme and the possibility of a joint venture. In the event, the GWR proved non-committal, but Fisher's conclusions regarding traffic prospects were much more positive. He took the view that the coal reserves of the upper part of the Treferig valley were sufficient, in themselves, to justify the cost of the railway, with the prospect of additional traffic when the deeper seams were mined. Although it was not possible for the TVR to expend its own capital on the Treferig Valley Railway, it could enter into a working agreement with the company under the Act of 1879. Accordingly, on 8th May, 1880 the TVR Board agreed to approach the Treferig promoters with a view to entering into such an arrangement. It was at this meeting that it was decided to build L&TVJR Railway No. 1, if a further extension of time was granted.

Following this decision, meetings took place between George Fisher and Tudor Crawshay, at which it was explained that the TVR was unable to expend its own capital on the Treferig Valley Railway. Instead, it was suggested that the Treferig promoters should build the line themselves, but with TVR backing. The form of this support was revealed at the TVR Board meeting on 28th May, 1881, when it was resolved to guarantee 4 per cent interest on the capital expended by the Treferig Company, from the date of completion of its railway. Draft agreement was reached on 8th June, 1881: in addition to the guarantee of interest on capital expended, the TVR was to be granted exclusive use of the Treferig Valley Railway, which it was to maintain and work. These terms were accepted by Treferig shareholders at meeting at the Royal Hotel, Cardiff, on 11th June, 1881 and by a Special General Meeting of the TVR on 14th July, 1881. All looked set for an early start on the new railway. On 26th July, 1881 George

Fisher and others interested in the new railway went over its route and two days later the authoritative *Western Mail* concluded that there was 'now a fair prospect that in a very short time the line will be commenced'.

This was not to be, however, as the GWR, not wishing to see the Treferig Valley Railway fall so easily to the TVR, despite its earlier indifference, objected when the TVR sought the approval of the Railway Commissioners for its draft agreement with the Treferig Company. In their ruling of 13th August, 1881, the Commissioners took the view that the power to enter into working and traffic agreements under the Treferig Valley Railway Act of 1879 did not cover the maintenance of the railway. They also considered that by offering to guarantee interest on the Treferig Company's capital, the TVR was, in effect, pledging its own funds towards the undertaking. Accordingly, they refused to approve the draft agreement. A fresh agreement, with the Treferig Company taking responsibility for maintenance and the guarantee of interest increased to 5 per cent, was hurriedly arranged and provisionally agreed on 20th October, 1881, being confirmed by a Special General Meeting of the TVR on 27th of that month. The revised agreement was accepted by the Railway Commissioners and, with this hurdle removed, work could commence on the Treferig Valley Railway. A ceremony of cutting the first sod took place on 23rd March, 1882, a special train bringing guests to the nearest point on the Common branch. On 20th April, 1882, the *South Wales Daily News* reported that work had commenced in 'right earnest', with about a score of men engaged on the line.

Despite the security provided by its agreement with the TVR, the Treferig Company was still unable to raise all its authorised capital. By November 1882, with work on the railway well advanced, and expected to be completed in two months, there was still a shortfall of £4,000 on the authorised capital of £15,000. In response to a further plea for assistance, the TVR Board agreed, at its meeting on 7th December, 1882, to provide a loan of £2,500 to enable the Treferig Company to complete its railway. This was increased to £3,000 on 11th January, 1883. With this additional support, work could continue on the new railway. At their half-yearly meeting on 24th February, 1883 Treferig shareholders were informed that their railway was fast approaching completion, indeed this was a matter of some urgency as 10,000 tons of coal were stockpiled at Glyn Colliery, awaiting the opening.

The opening of the Treferig Valley Railway was reported to its shareholders at the next half-yearly meeting on 30th August, 1883. The exact date of opening remains unclear, however; a later GWR source gives April 1883, while the subsequent lease of the Treferig line by the TVR was arranged to commence from the completion of the railway, which was given as 30th June, 1883, although this is likely to have been a notional date for the purpose of the agreement. The shareholders were told that their line had got off to a good start, with the Glyn Colliery sending out more coal than expected. The delay in opening the line was attributed to excessive zeal on the part of parish overseers regarding the design of two bridges. The cost of construction had exceeded estimates by £3,000 partly as a result of the higher standards of construction recommended by the TVR.

The Treferig Company's financial troubles persisted, however, despite the assistance provided by the TVR. On 27th September, 1883 the TVR Board was informed by Tudor Crawshay that his company was considering seeking further powers to raise additional capital. He also suggested that the TVR might wish to take up a lease of his company's railway. At their meeting on 8th November, 1883 the TVR Directors were informed that the Treferig Company had determined to seek fresh powers. At the TVR's request clauses were inserted in the Treferig Valley Railway Bill, deposited later that month, enabling a lease to be entered into, and providing for an extension of the Treferig Valley Railway to join the EVR and the EVER. This represented a revival of the TVR's ill-starred attempt to reach the Ogmore valley, and was probably designed to bring pressure on the GWR to reach agreement on the apportionment of receipts from traffic from the Ogmore valleys and possibly to dissuade that company from building its proposed line from Hendreforgan to Porth in the Rhondda valley, powers for which had been obtained in the previous Session. In the event, the extension lines were successfully opposed by the GWR and the Marquess of Bute, with the powers of the Treferig Valley Railway (Lease) Act of 14th July, 1884 being confined to the raising of additional capital and the confirmation of the agreement with the TVR, dated 5th May, 1884, to lease the undertaking.

This lease foreshadowed full-scale amalgamation of the two companies under the TVR (Amalgamations and Capital) Act of 26th August, 1889 (effective from 1st July, 1889). The Treferig Valley Railway did not, however, develop as its promoters had hoped. Glyn Colliery provided a worthwhile traffic on quite a substantial scale, with a siding capacity of 125 wagons and an ownership of 265 wagons in 1894, but was to remain the only significant colliery on the railway, while its subsequent closure was to deprive the line of most of its business at a stroke. Hopes for the exploitation of the deeper coal seams lower down the valley were never realised, so that the wider ambitions behind the building of the Treferig Valley Railway were never fulfilled.

Chapter Seven

Llantrisant Branches, Taff Vale Railway
1889-1922

By 1889 the Llantrisant branches of the TVR had reached their maximum extent, the system taking the form of a cross, intersecting at Common Branch Junction. By this date, however, one important feature had disappeared - the west curve at Common Branch Junction. The operating problems created by the loss of this line, with its potential as a direct link between Llantrisant No. 1 Railway and Glyn Colliery, were raised in March 1891 by TVR Traffic Manager, James Hurman, who noted that, as a result, traffic from Glyn Colliery to Penarth and Newport had to be worked via Llantrisant Junction and the TVR Main Line, rather than via the direct route provided by Llantrisant No. 1 Railway. Hurman asked that facilities be provided at Common Branch Junction to enable trains to make use of the direct route. Nothing was done, however, until 12th June, 1894, when substantial alterations were authorised at Common Branch Junction, at a cost of £1,660.

These alterations, important though they were, were but one part of a larger package of improvements authorised in 1894. The most far-reaching changes came with the adoption of the Electric Train Staff (ETS) system of single-line working between Llantrisant Junction and Maesaraul Junction, authorised on 27th July, 1894. This was followed, on 30th October, 1894, by approval for major alterations to signalling at Llantwit station.

Provisional sanction for the alterations at Common Branch Junction was granted by the Board of Trade on 19th October, 1894. The changes were inspected by Colonel Yorke, who, in his report dated 1st December, 1894, recommended approval for the revised arrangements. These involved the abolition of Common Branch Junction West, with Llantrisant No. 1 Railway being extended to run parallel to the main Llantrisant branch to Common Branch Junction East, where a new loop was provided. A new centrally positioned 36-lever signal cabin, known simply as 'Common Branch Junction', was provided to control all connections and signals at the junction.

The alterations resulting from the introduction of the ETS system were reported on by Colonel Yorke for the Board of Trade on 9th September, 1895, although TVR records indicate that they were carried out during 1894. The changes were extensive, with the signal cabins at Llantrisant Junction South, Taff Llantwit Colliery, Llantwit East, Wallsend, Cross Inn and Cottage Siding being abolished in favour of ground frames, unlocked by the ETS. At Llantwit station the signal cabins at Llantwit West and Llantwit Centre were replaced by a new central cabin.

The 1890s also saw a number of significant improvements to passenger facilities on the Llantrisant branch. A new station building for Cross Inn was authorised on 8th January, 1891, the tender of Thomas Taylor, of Pontypridd, being accepted on 5th March, 1891. The new building replaced the original structure, dating from 1869, and was typical of many provided on the TVR at this time, being constructed in yellow brick, with red brick detailing. The

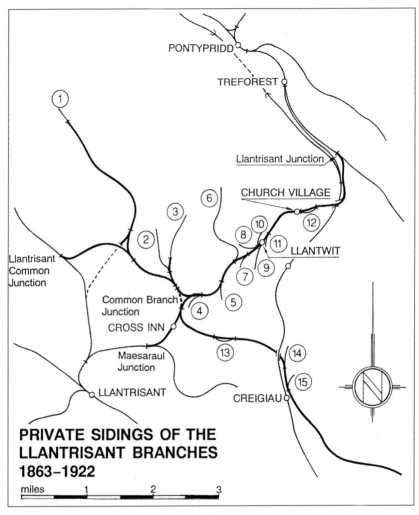

PONTYPRIDD

TREFOREST

①

Llantrisant Junction

⑥ CHURCH VILLAGE

③

⑩

⑧ ⑪ LLANTWIT

②

⑫

Llantrisant
Common
Junction

Common Branch
Junction ④ ⑤

CROSS INN

⑦ ⑨

Maesaraul
Junction ⑬ ⑭

⑮

LLANTRISANT CREIGIAU

**PRIVATE SIDINGS OF THE
LLANTRISANT BRANCHES
1863-1922**

miles   1   2   3

Key

Collieries
1. Glyn
2. Llantrisant Common
3. Gelynog / North Llantwit
4. Llantwit Main / Llantwit Red Ash
5. Llantwit Wallsend
6. Cwm Llantwit
7. Duffryn Llantwit
8. Tyn-y-nant / Ida / Llest Llantwit
9. Ystradbarwig / Garth Llantwit
   Llantwit Red Ash
10. Bryn

Collieries
11. Dihewyd / Llantwit / Rica / Llantwit
    Red Ash
12. Taff Llantwit
13. Tor-y-coed
14. South Cambria / South Glamorgam

Quarry
15. Creigiau

Not all sidings co-existed.

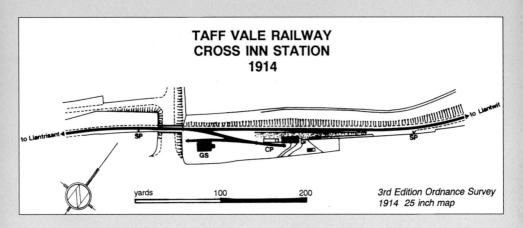

TAFF VALE RAILWAY
CROSS INN STATION
1914

to Llantrisant ◄

to Llantwit ►

SP

GS

CP

SP

yards 100 200

*3rd Edition Ordnance Survey
1914 25 inch map*

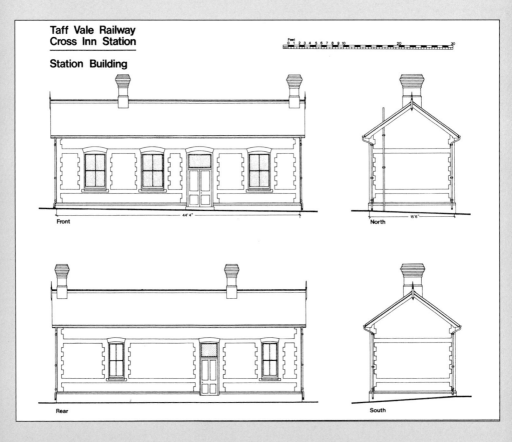

**Taff Vale Railway
Cross Inn Station**

Station Building

Feet 0 1 2 3 4 5 6 7 8 9 10 20 30

Front

44' 4"

North

15'6"

Rear

South

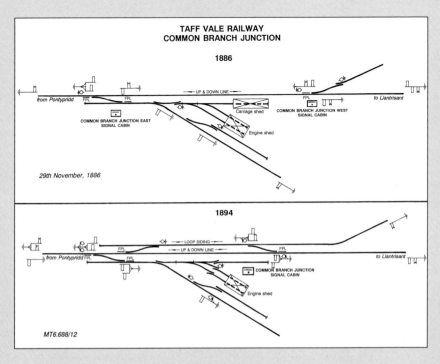

TAFF VALE RAILWAY
COMMON BRANCH JUNCTION

1886

from Pontypridd — FPL — FPL — ← UP & DOWN LINE →

COMMON BRANCH JUNCTION EAST
SIGNAL CABIN

Carriage shed

Engine shed

COMMON BRANCH JUNCTION WEST
SIGNAL CABIN

to Llantrisant

29th November, 1886

1894

← LOOP SIDING →
FPL — ← UP & DOWN LINE → — FPL
from Pontypridd FPL — FPL

COMMON BRANCH JUNCTION
SIGNAL CABIN

Engine shed

to Llantrisant

MT6.688/12

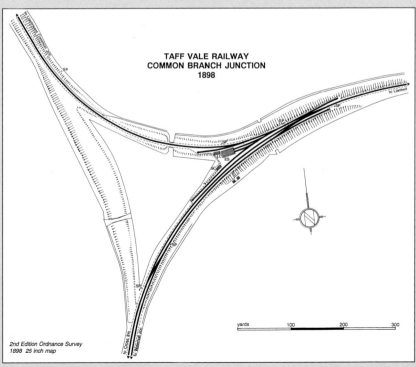

TAFF VALE RAILWAY
COMMON BRANCH JUNCTION
1898

to Llantwit

N

2nd Edition Ordnance Survey
1898 25 inch map

to Maindel Jcn.

to Cowbr. Jcn.

yards   100   200   300

platform at Church Village station was extended at about this time, following an accident in which a woman fell from a coach which had stopped short of the platform. Traffic growth at Church Village led to an extensive re-arrangement of passenger accommodation, this being approved on 12th October, 1898, at an estimated cost of £360.

A more positive approach to passenger services emerged following the appointment of Ammon Beasley, as TVR General Manager, in 1891. The following year saw the Llantrisant branch passenger service increased to five trains, each way, with a sixth return working being added in the following year.

An interesting passenger train development was foreshadowed in January 1892, when the Glyn Colliery Co. applied for the introduction of a workmen's train between Treferig Railway Junction (for Llantrisant) and Glyn Colliery. The service, to be provided on a contract basis, was approved by the TVR on 26th April, 1892, and was introduced without the benefit of Board of Trade sanction. All went well until 26th March, 1898, when the train was derailed at Treferig Siding, injuring one of the passengers. When the Board of Trade got to hear of this accident, it demanded an explanation, and called upon the TVR to submit the Treferig line for inspection, if it wished to continue operating the service. This cast serious doubt on the future of the workmen's train as inspection would certainly have brought with it additional costs necessary to bring the line up to passenger standards. Fortunately for the TVR and the Glyn Colliery miners, the Board of Trade withdrew its demand on being assured that the TVR accepted responsibility for the safe operation of the workmen's train, and would undertake certain precautions against accidents. In 1900 the Glyn workmen's train comprised three elderly four-wheeled coaches - a brake third and two all-thirds - with a total seating capacity of 130 passengers, together with a brake van.

The TVR's monopoly of the passenger traffic of the Llantwit Fardre district received a slight jolt on 16th March, 1896, when the Barry Railway opened a station at Efail Isaf, about a mile from Church Village, and served by trains between Porth and Barry. A more directly competitive service was introduced on 7th June, 1897, when Barry Railway trains started running between Pontypridd and Cardiff, via Efail Isaf, St Fagans and the GWR main line.

Freight traffic over the Llantrisant branches in the 1890s benefited from the opening of a number of private sidings. In 1890 a loop siding was installed to serve Taff Llantwit Colliery, just east of Church Village station, and controlled by a new six-lever signal cabin. The cabin and its associated signalling proved extremely short-lived, however, being swept away with the introduction of the ETS system in 1894. The colliery itself was a typically small-scale affair, connected to the siding by a tramway about ⅓ mile in length. Also typical was its life span of just over 10 years.

A rather more impressive span was achieved by the siding serving Creigiau Quarry, which opened in 1890, under a private siding agreement with Mr W. Thomas, dated 25th November, 1889. This agreement was transferred to Guest Keen and Nettlefords on 4th November, 1926, to Guest Keen and Baldwins Iron and Steel Co. on 3rd June, 1932, and eventually to the British Steel Corporation. The prospect of up to 200 tons of limestone daily from Creigiau Quarry to the

Common Branch Junction signal cabin *c.* 1910.

G. Croad Collection

Beddau Platform in TVR days, with excavation underway under the adjoining bridge. *D. Lewis*

Construction underway at Cwm Colliery *c.* 1911, with three TVR dropside open wagons in the centre of the picture. *WIMM*

A private owner wagon based on the Llantrisant branch. *HMRS*

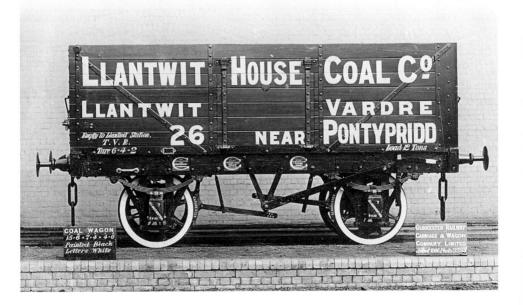

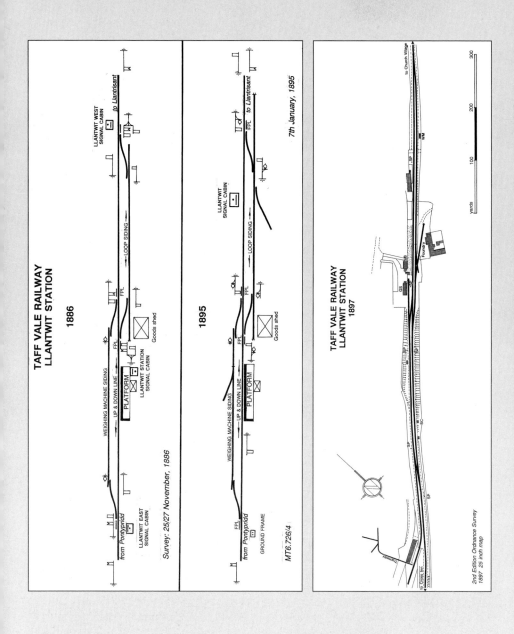

TAFF VALE RAILWAY
LLANTWIT STATION

1886

LLANTWIT WEST
SIGNAL CABIN

to Llantrisant

WEIGHING MACHINE SIDING

UP & DOWN LINE

FPL

LOOP SIDING

FPL

PLATFORM

from Pontypridd

LLANTWIT STATION
SIGNAL CABIN

Goods shed

LLANTWIT EAST
SIGNAL CABIN

Survey: 25/27 November, 1886

1895

LLANTWIT
SIGNAL CABIN

FPL   to Llantrisant

WEIGHING MACHINE SIDING

UP & DOWN LINE

FPL

LOOP SIDING

FPL

PLATFORM

from Pontypridd

GROUND FRAME

Goods shed

7th January, 1895

MT6.726/4

TAFF VALE RAILWAY
LLANTWIT STATION
1897

to Church Village

WM

SP

Foundry

GS

GS

SP

SP

SC

SP

Tramway

to Cross Inn

SP

yards   100   200   300

2nd Edition Ordnance Survey
1897 25 inch map

Llantwit station and staff in the early years of this century.   *C. Chapman Collection*

Station staff at Llantwit in TVR days.   *D. Lewis*

Church Village in TVR days, looking towards Llantwit Fardre.   *D. Lewis*

Church Village *c.* 1912 with a TVR auto-train composed of a purpose-built driving trailer and converted third class carriage, coupled to an 'M1' class 0-6-2T.

Welsh Industrial and Maritime Museum

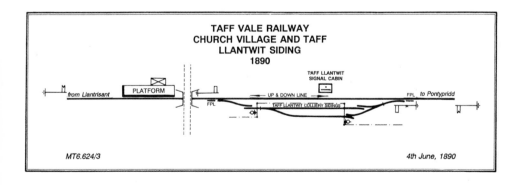

Cardiff-Dowlais Iron and Steel Works, at East Moors, Cardiff, then under construction, and opened on 4th February, 1891, prompted the TVR to approve, on 27th November, 1890, the provision of a new loop siding on Llantrisant No. 1 Railway, at Waterhall Junction.

In 1891 the Llantwit Red Ash Colliery Co., owned by Thomas Taylor of Pontypridd, opened Bryn Colliery on land adjoining the goods yard at Llantwit station. On 11th May, 1892 the TVR Directors were informed that the colliery company was about to mine the Llantwit No. 2 seam under the station, thereby threatening it with subsidence. Fortunately, this threat was averted with the closure of the Bryn Colliery in 1893, the colliery company transferring its activities to the nearby Ystradbarwig Colliery, which was opened up for the third time. The siding connection to the Llantrisant branch was again reinstated, being brought into use on 31st August, 1894. This third attempt did not meet with any more success than its predecessors, however, as the colliery closed as a result of flooding in 1896, the siding being lifted in 1897.

The relatively sparse traffic of Llantrisant No. 1 Railway received a welcome boost in 1897 with the opening of South Cambria Colliery, near Creigiau. A substantial undertaking by the standards of the area, with sidings capable of holding 178 wagons, South Cambria closed about 1906, but on 28th May, 1907 the TVR Engineer was instructed to put the sidings in good order in connection with the transfer of the private siding agreement to Messrs Montgomerie and Workman. The mine closed again about 1915, to be re-opened as the 'South Glamorgan Colliery', the new private siding agreement being dated 1st May, 1919. This agreement was eventually terminated on 1st February, 1928.

Train working over Llantrisant No. 1 Railway usually involved reversals at Waterhall Junction, and also, in the case of traffic bound for Cardiff, Radyr. In 1900 the TVR obtained powers for two curves, one at Waterhall Junction and the other at Radyr Quarry, which would have provided a direct route from the No. 1 Railway towards Cardiff. These powers were renewed under subsequent Acts but neither curve was constructed.

The new century saw the introduction of an additional branch passenger service from Llantrisant station. On 1st May, 1901, after many years of local agitation, the GWR commenced working passenger trains from Llantrisant to Penygraig, with an intermediate station at Tonyrefail. The introduction of this service followed the doubling of the EVR throughout, although only a single lead junction and trailing crossover were provided at Llantrisant Common Junction. Extensive alterations also took place at Llantrisant station, with a new bay for Penygraig trains being constructed on the up side. TVR trains, however, continued to cross the South Wales main line to reach the Cowbridge bay, on the down side.

The small settlement of Tonteg, to the east of Church Village, was some distance from the nearest station. On 4th November, 1902 the TVR refused a request from Llantwit Fardre Parish Council for a station to serve Tonteg. Despite this rejection, however, the need for passenger facilities was recognised in 1904, when plans were prepared for 'platforms' at various locations between Llantrisant Junction and Aberthaw, in connection with the introduction of steam railcars or 'motor cars' on the service. Having toyed with the idea of rail

The following are extracts from the TVR Working Timetable of 1st April, 1897.

ABERTHAW, COWBRIDGE, LLANTRISANT, WATERHALL, TREFERIG, AND LLANTRISANT JUNCTION.—UP.

No.	1	3		5		7		9		11		13		15		17		19		21
Description of Trains.	Carriages	Coke Ovens Express Goods		Pontypridd Passenger and Goods		Glyn to Roath Dock Through Goods		Local Goods		Pontypridd Passenger		Local Goods		Passenger		Passenger		Local Goods		
	C3	Z1		Z2		C3		C11a		Z2		Z1		Z3		Z3		X3		
Distance from Aberthaw. / STATIONS AND SIDINGS.	dep.	arr.	dep.	arr.	dep.	arr.	dep.	arr.	dep.	arr.	dep.	arr.	dep.	arr.	dep.	arr.	dep.	arr.	dep.	
M.CH. ABERTHAW		M D …	a.m. 5 35																	
0 67 ST. ATHAN ROAD																				
3 37 ST. MARY CHURCH ROAD																				
5 67 COWBRIDGE STATION				—	7 25					a.m. 9 55	9 53			a.m.	11 40			p.m.	p.m.	
Cowbridge Goods		M D 6 0		ST	7 31					10 2	9 56									
6 10 Cowbridge Junction			0 55	7 36	7 37					10 8	10 2							M D 10 25	10 15	
8 3 YSTRADOWEN				7 40 ST	7 45					10 13	10 8			11 45 ST	11 46			ST 10 35		
10 11 LLANHARRY										10 18	10 19 ST			11 51 ST	11 52			10 43	11 0	
11 36 LLANTRISANT STATION										10 22 ST	10 27			11 55 ST	x		12 35 ST	11 15	x1 35	
Mwyndy Junction														15a						
12 77 Maesaraul Junction																				
Brofiskin												11 40	11 35	Glyn Coal.						
Mwyndy Siding													11 45							
Bute Siding												11 50	11 55							
12 77 Maesaraul Junction		ST 7 3		7 51 ST	7 49							12 0	12 10	p.m.	p.m.	S T 12 39		S T	1 43	
13 18 Cottage Siding					7 52							To Cowbridge.				12 41	12 42			
13 46 CROSS INN STATION		ST 7 9		7 51 ST	7 54					S Tx 10 33	10 31				1 15					
Waterhall Junction								10 30	10 20											
1 75 St. Fagans Road								10 30	10 40						1 45					
4 42 Craigiu Quarries								10 50	11 10						x2 15					
4 74 South Cambria Colliery							8 10	11 15	11 25											
Glyn Colliery	7 0																			
18 8 Llan Common Junction	7 15					8 30	8 45													
16 52 Treferig Junction						9 0	9 15	11 30	12 15 To Glyn.		10 36			1 35						
14 11 Common Branch Junction														1 50	x2 15					
14 55 Walksend Siding																				
15 54 LLANTWIT STATION		ST 7 9	7 15	7 58 ST	7 59					S T 10 40	10 41			2 25	2 40	12 48 ST	12 49	S T 1 50x	1 49	
16 28 CHURCH VILLAGE		ST 7 15		8 1 ST	8 2					10 43	10 44					12 51	12 52	1 50x	2 10	
16 57 Taff Llantwit Colliery		7 25	7 30	ST	8 7											12 57		2 30	2 40	
18 17 Llantrisant Junction										S T 10 49				3 0	3 15					
Arrival at Destination		7 43		8 13						10 55				4 25		1 3		2 55		

STATIONS AND SIDINGS	23 Through Goods Z 2 & 3 arr.	23 dep.	25 Pontypridd Passenger Z 1 & 2 arr.	25 dep.	27 Cadtays to Glyn Mineral C 41 a arr.	27 dep.	29 Passenger and Goods Z 3 arr.	29 dep.	31 Pontypridd Passenger Z 2 arr.	31 dep.	33 Ystrad Local Goods X 7 arr.	33 dep.	35 Pontypridd Passenger Z 3 arr.	35 dep.	37 Glyn Coal C 41a arr.	37 dep.	39	41	41a
	p.m.	p.m.	p.m.	p.m.	p.m.	p.m.	p.m.	p.m.	p.m.	p.m.	p.m.	p.m.	p.m.	p.m.	p.m.	p.m.			
ABERTHAW	M D	12 50		2 30										6 45					
ST. ATHAN ROAD	12 55	1 5	2 32	2 33									6 47	6 48					
ST. MARY CHURCH ROAD	1 17	1 25	2 38	2 39	X S			5 8					6 53	6 54					
COWBRIDGE STN.			2 44	2 49									6 59	7 3					
Cowbridge Goods	1 35	S T 3 5	S T 2 50 x	2 54			S T	5 13					S T	7 8					
Cowbridge Jc.								5 10											
YSTRADOWEN			2 59	3 0			5 18			5 28			7 13	7 14					
LLANHARRY			3 3				5 21		S T				7 17x	7 22					
LLANTRISANT STN.	3 25			3 22									S T						
Mwyndy Jc.							29 a												
Maesaraul Jc.							Workmen's Train.		S T 5 34	5 32									
Brofiskin											6 15								
Mwynddy Sdg.											6 20								
Bute Sdg.									5 36			6 25		7 27					
Maesaraul Jc.			S T 3 28	3 26	3 50		C 41a	5 35			C R		S T 7 28	7 29					
Cottage Sdg.																			
CROSS INN STN.					4 50	5 0													
Waterhall Junction						To Glyn.													
St. Fagans Road								5 50											
Craigau Quarries																			
South Cambria Colliery					4 0										X S	6 40			
Glyn Colly.															6 55S	7 45			
Llantrisant Com. Jc									S T 5 37		6 35x	6 47	S T 7	7 31		8 0			
Treferig Jc.															8x10	8 40			
Common Branch Jc.									S T 5 41	5 42	6 57§	7 45	7 35§	7 36	9 0				
Wallsend Sdg.			3 35	3 36					5 44	5 45			7 38	7 39					
LLANTWIT STN.			3 38	3 39							8 5	8 20				9 10 10			
CHURCH VILLAGE																			
Taff Llantwit Colliery			S T 3 44						S T 5 50				S T 7	7 44					
Llantrisant Jc.																			
Arrival at Destination			3 50						5 56		10 15		7 50		11 10				

S To run Special to Wallsend if required.

M.CH.	STATIONS AND SIDINGS	2 Glyn Empties C 3 arr	dep	4 Glyn Workmen C 3 arr	dep	6 5.10 a.m. Coke Ovens Through Goods X 3 arr	dep	8 Glyn Empties C 3 arr	dep	10 8.38 a.m. Pontypridd Passenger Z 2 arr	dep	12 Glyn to Roath Dock Through Goods C 3 arr	dep	14 8.8 a.m. Coke Ovens Local Goods Z 1 arr	dep	16 Glyn Mineral C11a arr	dep	18 Aberthaw Local Goods Z 1 arr	dep	20	20a
—	Llantrisant Jc.	5 5	5 20			MD 5 35	6 0			ST	8 44			8 24S	MD 9 20						
1 65	Taff Llantwit Colliery																				
1 69	CHURCH VILLAGE		5 40								8 49				9 40						
2 13	LLANTWIT STN.	5 35				6 15	6 25			8 51	8 52			9 33							
3 42	Wallsend Sdg.						6 37							9 45	10 0						
4 6	Common Branch Jc.	5 50	6 0			ST				ST	8 55										
5 27	Treferig Jc.	6 10			6 20																
5 36	Llan. Common Jc.			6 40				7 50													
8 3	Glyn Colly.								7 30			9 0	9 15			12 25	12 15				
2 18	South Cambria Colliery											9 25	9 30				12 40				
2 50	Craigan Quarries											9 35	9 50			1 0					
5 17	St. Fagans Road											CR									
7 12	Waterhall Road											10 5	10 20								
11 18												10 53 To Roath Dk									
4 56	CROSS INN STN.					ST				8 57	9 0			10 27x	10 55						
4 79	Cottage Sdg.																				
5 20	Macsaraul Jc.													11 0	11 5						
	Bute Sdg.																				
6 58	Mwynddy Sdg.													11 10	11 15						
7 15	Broñskin													11 20							
5 20	Macsaraul Jc.																				
	Mwyndy Jc.																				
6 61	LLANTRISANT STN.					ST	6 50			ST	9 0							12 0	12 10		
8 6	LLANHARRY					7 0				9 4	9 9							12 20	12 50		
10 13	YSTRADOWEN					7 55	x8 5			9 12	9 13							12 55	1 5		
12 27	Cowbridge Jc.					8 10	8 20			9 18	9 19							1 10	1 15		
12 30	Cowbridge Goods					8 30				ST											
12 30	COWBRIDGE STN.									9 24	9 25							1 18	1 35		
17 60	ST. MARY CHURCH ROAD									9 30	9 30							1 45	1 50		
17 30	ST. ATHAN ROAD									9 35	9 36							1 59	2 10		
18 17	ABERTHAW									9 32									2 15		

NOTICE.—It is of the greatest importance that trains should be run TO TIME on this section.

No.	22		24		26		28		30		32		34		36		38		40	42
STATIONS AND SIDINGS.	11.20 a.m. Pontypridd Passenger. Z 2		1.50 p.m. Pontypridd Passenger. Z 3		2.10 p.m. Coke Ovens Local Goods. X 7		Glyn Empties. C 41a		4.20 p.m. Pontypridd Passenger. Z 2		Carriages. C 41a		Glyn Empties. C 41a		6.25 p.m. Pontypridd Passenger. Z 2		8.20 p.m. Pontypridd Passenger. Z 3			
Description of Trains.	arr. a.m.	dep. a.m.	arr. p.m.	dep. p.m.	arr. p.m.	dep. p.m.	arr. p.m.	dep. p.m.	arr. p.m.	dep. p.m.	arr. p.m.	dep. p.m.	arr. p.m.	dep. p.m.	arr. p.m.	dep. p.m.	arr. p.m.	dep. p.m.		
Llantrisant Jc.	S T	11 20	S T	1 50		3 0			S T	4 20					S T	6 25	S T	8 20		
Taff Llantwit Colliery					M D 2 40		X S						X S	6 5						
CHURCH VILLAGE	11 31	11 31	2 1	2 1		3 45			4 31	4 31					6 30	6 30		8 31		
LLANTWIT STN.	11 33	11 34	2 3	2 4	3 15x				4 33	4 34	X 8	5 15			6 39	6 39	8 33	8 34		
Wallsend Sdg.																				
Common Branch Jc.	S T	11 37	x2 7		S T	3 55			S T	4 37			X S	6	S T	6x42	S Tx	8 37		
Treferig Jc.																				
Llan. Common Jc.							4 50	5 0			X 8	5 30	6 20							
Glyn Colly.							5 10													
South Cambria Colliery																				
Craigau Quarries																				
St. Fagans Road																				
Waterhall Jc.																				
CROSS INN STN.	11 39	11 40	2 9	2 10		CR	28a		4 39	4 40	32a				6 44	6 45	8 39	8 40		
Cottage Sdg.																				
Maesaraul Jc.							Through Goods.				Passenger.									
Bute Sdg.							Z 3				Z 3									
Mwyndly Sdg.							p.m.	p.m.			p.m.	p.m.								
Brofiskin								4 0			5 40						S T	8 42		
Maesaraul Jc.	S T	11 42	S T	2 12	S T	4 5			S T	4 42	5 43	5 40			S T	6 47	S T			
Mwyndly Jc.	S T				S T				S T		5 49	5 44			S T		S T			
LLANTRISANT STN.	11 48	x12 5	2 16	2 30	4 15		8 T		4 46		5 50	5 50			6 51x	7 25	8 46	8 51		
LLANHARRY	12 8	12 9	2 33	2 34			4 20								7 28	7 29	8 54	8 55		
YSTRADOWEN	12 14	12 15	2 39	2 40			S T				S T				7 34	7 35	9 0	9 1		
Cowbridge Jc.	S T		S T	2 45x											S T					
Cowbridge Goods...			2 49								5 55	6 0					9			
COWBRIDGE STN.	12 20	12 22	2 50									6 5			7 40		9			
ST. MARY CHURCH ROAD	12 32	12 27	2 33								6 10	6 11								
ST. ATHAN ROAD	12 32	12 33									6 13									
ABERTHAW	12 35										S T									

PONTYPRIDD, COWBRIDGE AND ABERTHAW.—TO AND FROM T.V.R. AND G.W.R. STATIONS.

UP TRAINS.   WEEK DAYS.

		a.m.	a.m.	p.m.	p.m.	p.m.	p.m.
Aberthaw	dep.		9 50		2 15		6 45
St. Athan Road ..	„		9 53		2 20		6 48
St. Mary Church Rd..	„		9 59		2 31		6 54
Cowbridge .. .. {arr.		a.m.	10 4	p.m.	2 39	p.m.	6 59
Cowbridge .. .. {dep.		7 25	10 5	12 20	2 46	5 8	7 3
Ystradowen	„	7 31	10 10	12 26	2 54	5 13	7 8
Llanharry	„	7 37	10 16	12 32	3 0	5 19	7 14
Llantrisant	arr.	7 40	10 19	12 35	3 3	5 22	7 17

G.W. Railway

			a.m.	a.m.	p.m.		p.m.
Porthcawl ..	dep.		8 30	10 22	2 5		6 27
Maesteg ..	„		7 22	10 14	1 27		6 15
Tondu ..	„		7 40	10 32	1 45		6 33
Bridgend ..	„		8 53	10 51	2 52		6 57
Llantrisant ..	arr.		9 14	11 14	3 16		7 11

		a.m.	a.m.	p.m.	p.m.	p.m.	p.m.
Llantrisant, (G.W.) ..	dep.	7 45	10 24	12 47	3 22	5 25	7 22
Cross Inn (for Llantrisant)	„	7 52	10 31	12 54	3 29	5 32	7 29
Llantwit	„	7 59	10 38	1 1	3 36	5 39	7 36
Church Village ..	„	8 2	10 41	1 4	3 39	5 42	7 39
Treforest	„	8 10	10 49	1 12	3 47	5 50	7 47
Pontypridd	arr.	8 13	10 52	1 15	3 50	5 53	7 50

Main Line

		a.m.	a.m.	a.m.	p.m.	p.m.	p.m.	p.m.	p.m.	p.m.	p.m.
Pontypridd	dep.	8 20	10 55	11 8	1 23	4 4	4 13	6 11	6 23	8 0	8 10
Treforest	„			11 12	1 27		4 17		6 27		8 14
Walnut Tree Bridge	arr.	8 30		11 21	1 36		4 27		6 36		8 22
Radyr	„	8 35		11 26	1 41		4 32		6 41		8 28
Llandaff for Whitchurch	„	8 41	11 13	11 32	1 47	4 22	4 38	6 29	6 47	8 18	8 34
Cardiff (Queen St.)	„	8 47	11 19	11 38	1 53	4 28	4 44	6 35	6 53	8 24	8 40

Rhondda Branches

		a.m.	a.m.		p.m.		p.m.		p.m.		p.m.
Pontypridd ..	dep.	8 36	11 19		1 30		4 19		6 28		8 3
Porth ..	arr.	8 46	11 29		1 40		4 29		6 38		8 13
Ferndale	„	9 13	11 55		2 5		4 54		7 1		8 41
Ystrad	„	9 6	11 49		2 0		4 49		6 58		8 33
Treherbert ..	„	9 16	11 59		2 10		4 59		7 8		8 43

Aberdare and Merthyr

		a.m.	a.m.		p.m.		p.m.		p.m.		p.m.
Pontypridd ..	dep.	8 23	11 4		1 48		4 8		6 12		8 13
Abercynon ..	arr.	8 29	11 10		1 54		4 14		6 18		8 19
Aberdare	„	9 0	11 42		2 24		4 45		6 49		8 49
Merthyr	..	9 4	11 45		2 27		4 50		6 52		8 50

NO SUNDAY TRAINS

DOWN TRAINS   WEEK DAYS.

Merthyr, Aberdare, Abercynon

		a.m.	a.m.	a.m.	a.m.	p.m.	p.m.	p.m.	p.m.	p.m.	p.m.	p.m.
Merthyr	dep.	7 52			10 30	12 45	3 35		5 45	7 20		
Aberdare ..	„	7 55			10 30	12 45	3 35		5 45	7 20		
Abercynon.. ..	„	8 20			10 59	1 14	4 4		6 14	7 49		
Pontypridd ..	arr.	8 26			11 5	1 20	4 10		6 20	7 55		

Rhondda Branches

		a.m.	a.m.	a.m.	a.m.	p.m.	p.m.	p.m.	p.m.	p.m.	p.m.	p.m.
Treherbert ..	dep.	7 40			10 15	1 5	3 25		5 30	7 30		
Ystrad ..	„	7 50			10 25	1 15	3 35		5 40	7 40		
Ferndale	„	7 46			10 21	1 11	3 31		5 36	7 31		
Porth	„	8 7			10 42	1 32	3 52		5 57	7 57		
Pontypridd.. ..	arr.	8 16			10 51	1 41	4 1		6 6	8 6		

Main Line

		a.m.	a.m.	a.m.	a.m.	p.m.	p.m.	p.m.	p.m.	p.m.	p.m.	p.m.
Cardiff (Queen St.)	dep.	7 50	8 10	10 30	10 55	1 15	3 35	3 55	5 57	7 30	7 50	
Llandaff for Whitchurch	„	7 57		10 37		1 22	3 42		6 4	7 37		..V
Radyr ..	„	8 1		10 41		1 26	3 46		6 8	7 41		
Walnut Tree Bridge	„	8 6		10 46		1 31	3 51		6 13	7 46		
Treforest ..	arr.	8 16	8 29	10 56		1 41	4 1		6 24	7 56		
Pontypridd.. ..	„				11 15	1 44		4 15		8 10		

		a.m.		a.m.	p.m.	p.m.	p.m.	p.m.	p.m.
Pontypridd	dep.	8 33		11 20	1 55	4 20	6 30	8 20	
Treforest	„	8 37		11 24	1 59	4 24	6 34	8 24	
Church Village	„	8 45		11 32	2 7	4 32	6 42	8 32	
Llantwit	„	8 48		11 35	2 10	4 35	6 45	8 35	
Cross Inn (for Llantrisant)	„	8 54		11 41	2 16	4 41	6 51	8 41	
Llantrisant (G.W.) ..	arr.	9 0		11 47	2 22	4 47	6 57	8 47	

G.W. Railway

		a.m.	a.m.	p.m.	p.m.	p.m.	p.m.	p.m.
Llantrisant.. ..	dep.	10 36	12 0	3 18	5 32		10 42	
Bridgend ..	arr.	10 55	12 21	3 38	5 53		10 59	
Tondu ..	„	11 19	2 27	5 2	7 49			
Maesteg	„	11 40	2 58	5 23	8 10			
Perthcawl ..	„	11 36	12 55	4 2	6 25			

		a.m.	a.m.	p.m.	p.m.	p.m.	p.m.	p.m.
Llantrisant	dep.	9 5	12 5	2 30	5 40	7 25	8 51	
Llanharry ..	„	9 9	12 9	2 34	5 44	7 29	8 55	
Ystradowen ..	„	9 15	12 15	2 40	5 50	7 35	9 1	
Cowbridge . .. {arr.		9 20	12 22	2 49	5 55	7 40	9 6	
Cowbridge . .. {dep.		9 22	12 30		6 0			
St. Mary Church Road	„	9 27	12 42		6 5			
St. Athan Road	„	9 32	12 52		6 11			
Aberthaw ..	arr.	9 35	12 59		6 14			

NO SUNDAY TRAINS

Extract from the TVR Public Timetable, June 1899.

level platforms, the TVR opted for raised platforms, including one at Tonteg. Tonteg Platform opened on 1st May, 1905, with the introduction of motor cars between Pontypridd and Aberthaw. It was some distance from the village it was intended to serve, at the foot of a steep hill, and comprised a single 40 ft long platform without any form of shelter. Coincidentally, the Barry Railway (ByR) opened its own platform, somewhat nearer the village, on the same day. This was served by ByR motor cars, running between Pontypridd and Cardiff, via St Fagans. This service was not a success, however, with the cars being withdrawn in favour of conventional locomotive and coaches working, and Tonteg Platform (ByR) closing on 31st May, 1905.

Interestingly, the TVR also considered introducing an indirect service between Pontypridd and Cardiff, via the main Llantrisant branch and the Llantrisant No. 1 Railway. Reports of such a proposal appeared in local newspapers in July and October 1904, and on 17th May, 1906, TVR Directors examined possible sites for motor-car platforms on Llantrisant No. 1 Railway.

With the introduction of the motor cars, the passenger service over the Llantrisant branch was increased to nine workings, each way. A single locomotive and coaches return working was retained, however, to handle tail traffic, which the cars were not permitted to convey over the steeply graded single line. This train did not call at Tonteg Platform. The frequency of the service was constrained by the lack of suitable passing places between Llantrisant Junction and Mwyndy Junction. To facilitate the operation of a more intensive service, modifications to signalling, together with the provision of facing point locks in appropriate positions, were carried out in 1906 at Maesaraul Junction (in conjunction with renewal of the layout by the GWR) and Common Branch Junction, to enable the loops to be used as passing places for passenger workings. In 1910 similar modifications were carried out at Llantwit, enabling up passenger trains to make use of the former goods loop, to the west of the passenger station, for passing purposes.

After repeated requests for an early morning workmen's train from Llantrisant to Pontypridd, the TVR finally bowed to public pressure in July 1904 and agreed to an experimental service. In view of its uncertain prospects, however, higher fares were to be charged than applied to similar services elsewhere on the TVR. The service continued beyond its 3 months experimental period, but does not appear to have been particularly remunerative, given the repeated reviews of its performance. Indeed, it appeared doomed in November 1909, when the TVR gave notice of its intention to withdraw the service. At the last minute, however, this decision was rescinded and the service was retained.

The passenger service was modified slightly in 1906, when a mid-morning motor car return trip was replaced by a locomotive and coaches working. In addition, a 4.42 pm Pontypridd to Llantrisant car was introduced, returning empty from Llantrisant. Another short working was added in May 1907, in the form of an 8.12 am car from Pontypridd to Cross Inn, returning at 8.40 am. With the introduction of auto-trains in 1908, the locomotive and coaches workings were withdrawn. The service was then shared between a motor-car and an auto-train, the latter being permitted to convey tail traffic over the Llantrisant branch.

TRAINS AND STEAM MOTOR CARS.
Aberthaw, Cowbridge, Llantrisant and Pontypridd Section.

UP.

	A.M.	A.M. Car	A.M. Car	A.M.	A.M. (Tues. only)	A.M. Car	P.M.	P.M. Car	P.M. Car	P.M.	P.M. Car	P.M.	P.M. Car
Aberthaw ... dep	...	...	8 5	9 45	11 40	...	1 14	...	4 37	...	...	8 13	...
St. Athan Road ,,	...	...	8 8	9 48	11 43	...	1 17	...	4 40	...	...	8 16	...
Llanbethery Platform ,,	...	...	8 11	...	11 46	...	1 20	...	4 43	...	...	8 19	...
St. Mary Church Road ,,	...	...	8 17	9 54	11 52	...	1 26	...	4 49	...	...	8 25	...
St. Hilary Platform ,,	...	...	8 20	...	11 55	...	1 29	...	4 52	...	...	8 28	...
Cowbridge ... arr	...	...	8 25	9 59	12 0	...	1 34	...	4 57	...	...	8 33	...
Cowbridge ... dep	7 15	...	8 28	10 3		12 5	1 38	2 55	5 0	...	6 45	8 36	...
Aberthin Platform ,,	...	...	8 31	...		12 8	1 41	2 58	5 3	...	6 48	8 39	...
Trerhyngyll & Maendy ,,	...	...	8 33	...		12 10	1 43	3 0	5 5	...	6 50	8 41	...
Ystradowen ... ,,	7 21	...	8 38	10 9		12 15	1 48	3 5	5 10	...	6 55	8 46	...
Llanharry ... ,,	7 27	...	8 43	10 15		12 20	1 53	3 10	5 15	...	7 0	8 51	...
Llantrisant for G.W.R. arr	7 30	...	8 47	10 18		12 24	1 57	3 14	5 19	...	7 4	8 55	...
Llantrisant G.W.R. dep	8 22	...	9 16	11 27		...	12 56	2 12	3 22	5 35	...	7 18	9 30 ...
Cardiff G.W.R. ... arr	8 52	...	9 42	11 55		...	1 15	2 30	3 50	6 2	...	7 45	9 52 ...
Llantrisant for G.W.R. dep	7 37	...	8 52	10 28		...	12 50	2 32	3 40	5 23	6 3	7 24	9 0 ...
Cross Inn for Llantris't ,,	7 45	8 40	9 0	10 35		...	12 57	2 39	3 50	5 33	6 10	7 31	9 7 ...
Llantwit ... ,,	7 53	8 48	9 8	10 43		...	1 5	2 47	3 58	5 41	6 18	7 39	9 15 ...
Church Village ... ,,	7 56	8 51	9 11	10 46		...	1 8	2 50	4 1	5 44	6 21	7 42	9 18 ...
Tonteg Platform ... ,,	...	8 55	9 15	...		...	1 12	2 54	4 5	5 48	6 25	7 46	9 22 ...
Treforest ... ,,	8 4	9 0	9 20	10 54		...	1 17	2 59	4 11	5 54	6 31	7 51	9 28 ...
Pontypridd Junction arr	8 7	9 3	9 23	10 57		...	1 20	3 2	4 14	5 57	6 34	7 54	9 31 ...
Connecting trains leave Pontypridd for—													
Aberdare ... at	8 12	...	9 35	11 13		...	1 47	3 23	4 27	6 12	...	8 17	10 9 ...
Rhondda Branches ,,	8 38	...	9 35	11 25		...	1 33	3 30	4 32	6 30	...	8 8	10 10 ...
Merthyr ... ,,	8 26	...	9 35	11 13		...	1 47	3 23	4 27	6 12	...	8 17	10 9 ...
Cardiff ... ,,	8 20	9 9	9 58	11 3		...	1 43	3 10	4 29	6 8	7 1	8 0	9 44 ...

(Vertical note in the A.M. column: "Tues. only")

DOWN.

	A.M. Car	A.M.	A.M. Car	A.M.	P.M. Car	P.M. Car	P.M. Car	P.M. Car	P.M. Car	P.M. Car	P.M. Car	P.M. Car
Connecting trains arr. Pontypridd from—												
Cardiff ... at	...	8 21	9 29	11 9	1 29	2 51	4 24	...	6 9	7 44	8 15	9 20 ...
Merthyr ... ,,	...	8 25	9 6	11 11	1 21	3 6	4 26	...	6 19	...	7 57	9 41 ...
Rhondda ... ,,	7 0	8 16	9 55	11 0	1 39	3 1	4 54	5 86	6 6	6 59	8 6	9 36 ...
Aberdare ... ,,	...	8 25	9 6	11 11	1 21	3 6	4 26	...	6 19	6 51	7 57	9 41 ...
Pontypridd Junction dep	8 12	8 31	10 3	11 27	1 46	3 15	4 35	5 15	6 25	7 52	8 20	10 5 ...
Treforest ... ,,	8 16	8 35	10 7	11 31	1 50	3 19	4 39	5 19	6 29	7 56	8 24	10 9 ...
Tonteg Platform ... ,,	8 23	...	10 14	...	1 57	3 26	4 46	5 26	6 36	3 8	8 31	10 16 ...
Church Village ... ,,	8 27	8 43	10 18	11 39	2 1	3 30	4 50	5 31	6 41	8 8	8 36	10 20 ...
Llantwit ... ,,	8 30	8 46	10 21	11 42	2 4	3 33	4 53	5 34	6 43	8 11	8 39	10 23 ...
Cross Inn for Llantris't ,,	8 37	8 52	10 28	11 49	2 11	3 40	5 0	5 41	6 50	...	8 46	10 30 ...
Llantrisant for G.W.R. arr	...	8 58	10 33	11 55	2 16	3 45	5 4	5 46	6 55		8 51	10 35 ...
Cardiff G.W.R. ... dep	...	7 38	10 20	11 55	1 5	2 50	...	5 10	6 50		...	9 35 ...
Llantrisant for G.W.R. arr	...	8 7	10 40	12 14	1 31	3 18	...	5 38	7 11		...	10 4 ...
Llantrisant for G.W.R. dep	...	9 5	10 45	12 27	2 19	3 48	...	5 51	7 26		9 3	10 40 ...
Llanharry ... ,,	...	9 9	10 51	12 31	2 25	3 54	...	5 57	7 32		9 9	10 46 ...
Ystradowen ... ,,	...	9 15	10 56	12 37	2 30	3 59	...	6 2	7 37		9 14	10 51 ...
Trerhyngyll & Maendy ,,	...	...	10 59	...	2 33	4 2	...	6 5	7 40		9 17	10 54 ...
Aberthin Platform ... ,,	...	...	11 1	...	2 35	4 4	...	6 7	7 42		9 19	10 56 ...
Cowbridge ... arr	Car	9 20	11 4	12 43	2 38	4 7	...	6 10	7 45		9 22	10 59 ...
Cowbridge ... dep	7 40	9 22	11* 8	12 48		4 11	...	7 48	...		...	...
St. Hilary Platform ... ,,	7 45	...	11*13	12 53		4 16	...	7 53	...		...	...
St. Mary Church Road ,,	7 48	9 27	11*16	12 56		4 19	...	7 56	...		...	...
Llanbethery Platform ,,	7 54	...	11*22	1 2		4 25	...	8 2	...		...	...
St. Athan Road ... ,,	7 57	9 33	11*25	1 5		4 28	...	8 5	...		...	...
Aberthaw ... arr	7 59	9 35	11*27	1 7		4 30	...	8 7	...		...	...

(Vertical notes in the DOWN columns: "Sats. only" and "Car".)

Tuesday only.   **NO SUNDAY SERVICE.**

Extract from the TVR Public Timetable, May 1907.

The introduction of the motor-car service led to requests for additional platforms in areas not well-served by existing stations. In September 1905 the TVR rejected a request from the Llantrisant and Llantwit Fardre Parish Councils for a platform at Wallsend, midway between Llantwit station and Common Branch Junction. An interesting, but again unsuccessful, request was that made in March 1909 by Cardiff City Council for a platform at Capel Llaniterne, on Llantrisant No. 1 Railway, intended to serve about 120 persons expected to occupy land there under the Small Holdings Act 1907. A second request for a platform at Wallsend was rejected in May 1909, but the matter was reconsidered in the following September and approved at an estimated cost of £231. Following the suggestion of a local schoolmaster, it was agreed that this platform should be named 'Beddau', after the village about 1 mile to the north, which was to grow rapidly following the opening of Cwm Colliery. Beddau Platform opened in July 1910, being served by all motor cars and auto-trains between Pontypridd and Llantrisant. The platform itself was only 40 ft long, however, and this led to an objection from the Board of Trade when, on 8th August, 1910, it was reported on following inspection. Colonel Druitt, the Board of Trade Inspector, insisted that it be lengthened if it was to continue to be served by two-coach auto-trains. This was authorised, together with the lengthening of Tonteg Platform, in October 1910, both platforms being increased to 130 ft in length. Shelter for the long-suffering patrons of Beddau and Tonteg Platforms was authorised in December of that year, following a request from Llantwit Fardre Parish Council.

The 1908 timetable represented the high point of the passenger train service on the Llantrisant branch in TVR days. In 1910 a Saturdays-only short working to Llantwit was withdrawn, followed in 1914 by the cutting back to Llantwit, on Mondays to Fridays, of the early evening Pontypridd to Llantrisant service.

Regular services were augmented by a variety of excursions. These included trains from Llantrisant branch stations to TVR and other destinations, and others over the line *en route* to Cowbridge for the races or the Show, and to Aberthaw for the seaside. The most important single source of such traffic, however, was the many excursions from various valley communities to Porthcawl. TVR coaches worked through, with GWR engines taking over at Llantrisant for the run along the South Wales main line to Pyle and from there over the sharply curved single track branch to Porthcawl. Special tickets and facilities were also widely available, including market tickets to Pontypridd on Wednesdays and Saturdays, to Cardiff (via Treforest) on Wednesdays, and to Cowbridge on Tuesdays.

The increase in the output of the South Wales coalfield in the years up to World War I was also reflected in developments in the area served by the Llantrisant branches. Rising demand encouraged the sinking of otherwise marginal pits, usually small in scale and short on life span. In February 1900 the TVR accepted a request from Messrs Hood and Richards for a private siding to serve Tor-y-Coed Colliery on Llantrisant No. 1 Railway. A private siding agreement, dated 31st December, 1909, was later entered into with the Torycoed Colliery Co. A siding to another small colliery, Llantwit Red Ash, owned initially by Messrs Thomas and Evans of Porth, and adjoining Llantwit station,

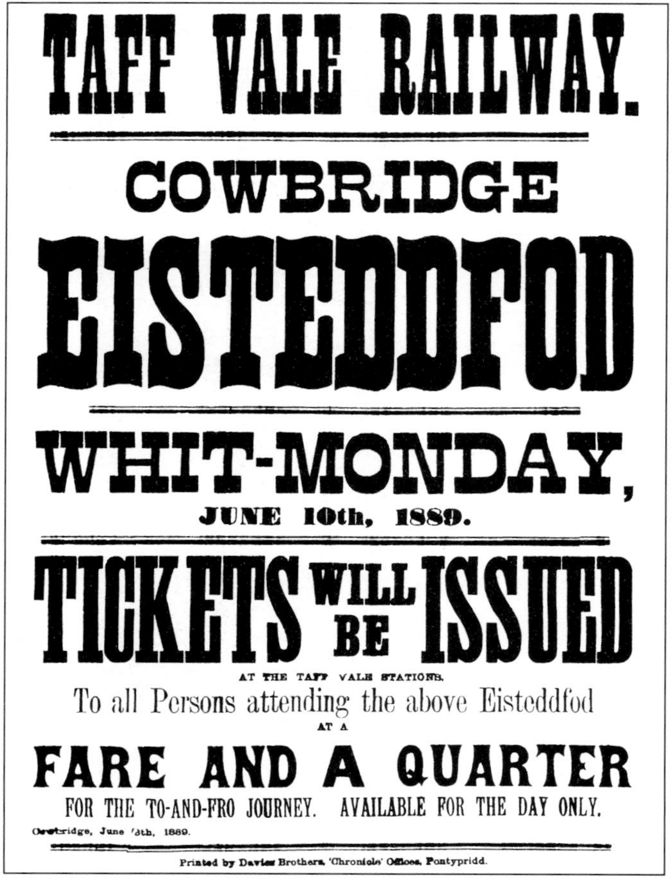
TAFF VALE RAILWAY.

COWBRIDGE EISTEDDFOD

WHIT-MONDAY,

JUNE 10th, 1889.

TICKETS WILL BE ISSUED

AT THE TAFF VALE STATIONS.

To all Persons attending the above Eisteddfod

AT A

FARE AND A QUARTER

FOR THE TO-AND-FRO JOURNEY. AVAILABLE FOR THE DAY ONLY.

Cowbridge, June 3th, 1889.

Printed by Davies Brothers, 'Chronicle' Offices, Pontypridd.

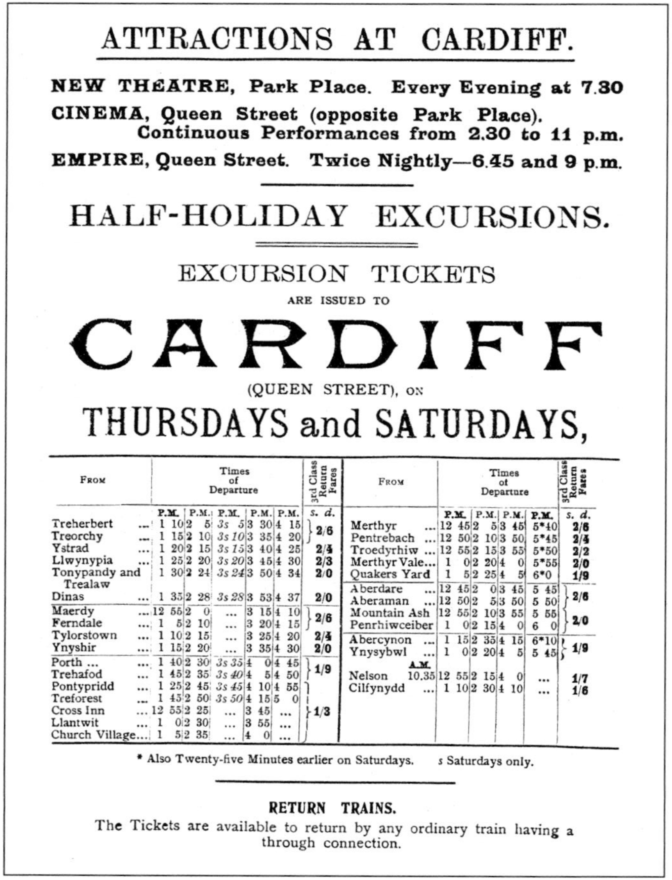
ATTRACTIONS AT CARDIFF.

NEW THEATRE, Park Place. Every Evening at 7.30

CINEMA, Queen Street (opposite Park Place). Continuous Performances from 2.30 to 11 p.m.

EMPIRE, Queen Street. Twice Nightly—6.45 and 9 p.m.

HALF-HOLIDAY EXCURSIONS.

EXCURSION TICKETS

ARE ISSUED TO

CARDIFF

(QUEEN STREET), ON

THURSDAYS and SATURDAYS,

From	Times of Departure P.M.	P.M.	P.M.	P.M.	P.M.	3rd Class Return Fares s. d.
Treherbert ...	1 10	2 5	3s 5	3 30	4 15	2/6
Treorchy ...	1 15	2 10	3s 10	3 35	4 20	
Ystrad ...	1 20	2 15	3s 15	3 40	4 25	2/4
Llwynypia ...	1 25	2 20	3s 20	3 45	4 30	2/3
Tonypandy and Trealaw	1 30	2 24	3s 24	3 50	4 34	2/0
Dinas ...	1 35	2 28	3s 28	3 53	4 37	2/0
Maerdy ...	12 55	2 0	...	3 15	4 10	2/6
Ferndale ...	1 5	2 10	...	3 20	4 15	
Tylorstown ...	1 10	2 15	...	3 25	4 20	2/4
Ynyshir ...	1 15	2 20	...	3 35	4 30	2/0
Porth	1 40	2 30	3s 35	4 0	4 45	1/9
Trehafod ...	1 45	2 35	3s 40	4 5	4 50	
Pontypridd ...	1 25	2 45	3s 45	4 10	4 55	1/3
Treforest ...	1 45	2 50	3s 50	4 15	5 0	
Cross Inn ...	12 55	2 25	...	3 45	...	
Llantwit ...	1 0	2 30	...	3 55	...	
Church Village...	1 5	2 35	...	4 0	...	

From	Times of Departure P.M.	P.M.	P.M.	P.M.	3rd Class Return Fares s. d.
Merthyr ...	12 45	2 5	3 45	5*40	2/6
Pentrebach ...	12 50	2 10	3 50	5*45	2/4
Troedyrhiw ...	12 55	2 15	3 55	5*50	2/2
Merthyr Vale...	1 0	2 20	4 0	5*55	2/0
Quakers Yard	1 5	2 25	4 5	6*0	1/9
Aberdare ...	12 45	2 0	3 45	5 45	2/6
Aberaman ...	12 50	2 5	3 50	5 50	
Mountain Ash	12 55	2 10	3 55	5 55	2/0
Penrhiwceiber	1 0	2 15	4 0	6 0	
Abercynon ...	1 15	2 35	4 15	6*10	1/9
Ynysybwl ...	1 0	2 20	4 5	5 45	
Nelson A.M. 10.35	12 55	2 15	4 0	...	1/7
Cilfynydd ...	1 10	2 30	4 10	...	1/6

* Also Twenty-five Minutes earlier on Saturdays. *s* Saturdays only.

RETURN TRAINS.

The Tickets are available to return by any ordinary train having a through connection.

Posters showing details of TVR excursions tickets. The first for Cowbridge Eisteddfod in 1889, the poster for half-holiday excursions to Cardiff dates from 1909.

John Lyons and Author

Two views of Tor-y-coed Colliery, taken from picture postcards. *Pope/Parkhouse Archive*

Treferig Branch.

TREFERIG AND CASTELLAU SIDINGS.—Station to station traffic in truck loads only is dealt with at these sidings.

The points are facing for trains running towards Glyn Colliery. They are padlocked, and the key is the train staff for the section.

Traffic for these sidings must be taken up in front of the engine.

(2042)

TREFERIG JUNCTION.—The Junction points are connected to a ground frame with one lever. When the lever is in the normal position, the points will lie for the Treferig Branch, and must be locked in that position. The key is the train staff for the section.

Llantrisant and Cowbridge Branches.

1. The principal gradients on this section are as follow :—

From Llantrisant Junction	...	...	1 in 40 rise for about a mile towards Llantwit.
„ Common Branch Junction	...	...	1 in 50 fall to Cross Inn Station.
„ Cross Inn Station	...	...	1 in 40 fall to Maesaraul Junction.
„ Llanharry	...	...	1 in 45 rise towards Ystradowen
„ Ystradowen	...	...	1 in 50 fall towards Cowbridge.

2. The line is single, except between Cowbridge Road Crossing and Llantrisant, and worked by Electric Staff between Llantrisant Junction and Cowbridge Road Crossing, and between Llantrisant and Cowbridge Junction.

3. The speed of goods, mineral and ballast trains, when descending these gradients, must not exceed **eight** miles per hour.

4. Passenger trains must not exceed **booked speed**.

5. The maximum loads for goods and mineral trains with one engine will be as under :—

When ascending Llantrisant Junction and Cross Inn gradients, ten 10-ton loaded wagons : for the other banks, twelve loaded 10-ton wagons or equivalent thereto, except between Common Branch Junction and Llantwit, where the maximum load for one engine will be 15 loaded 10-ton wagons or equivalent thereto, and between Llantrisant and Llanharry where the load for one engine will be 13 loaded 10-ton vehicles or equivalent thereto.

6. Trains having the assistance of a bank engine may take double the above loads, but no load must exceed 50 wagons, whether laden or empty.

7. When descending these gradients with one engine, equal to 30 loaded 10-ton wagons ; but when assisted by a second engine the load must not exceed 50 wagons and van.

8. When ascending the inclines between Maesaraul Junction and Common Branch Junction, also between Llantrisant Junction and Llantwit Station, the assistant engine must be at the rear of each train.

9. Every passenger train on this section must be formed with a van at each end, and a guard must ride in each van, except where otherwise ordered by the Superintendent of the Line.

10. A post, painted white, is fixed at the top of the bank nearest Llantrisant Junction, at which every Up goods, mineral, and ballast train must **stop dead**.

Horse Boxes and extra Vehicles, Llantrisant and Cowbridge Section.

Horse boxes, carriage trucks, etc., must not be accepted for conveyance in either direction by motor cars between Llantrisant and Pontypridd, as the motor cars cannot convey such vehicles over the heavy gradients. In the case of the Auto Train, however, the conveyance of such vehicles may be specially arranged upon communication with the Superintendent of the Line. One horse box or carriage truck may be attached to a Motor Car for conveyance between Llantrisant and Cowbridge in either direction.

Llantrisant No. 1 Railway.

1 When travelling from Waterhall Junction to Common Branch Junction the wagons must be pushed in front of the engine, and when travelling in the reverse direction, they must be drawn.

2. There is a loop at Waterhall Junction for putting off Down traffic or crossing trains.

3. St. Pagans Road Siding facing points for Up trains are padlocked. This siding is to accommodate mileage traffic only. The safety points are connected with a ground frame which is locked and unlocked by the train staff. (T. 71,469.)

4. **Pantygored Siding.**—The points are facing for Up trains, and the siding is used for mileage traffic only.

5. There is a turn over stop-block inside the catch-points fitted with a bolt and padlock.

6. Trainmen using this siding must, before leaving, throw over the turn-over stop block across the line and lock it so as to prevent vehicles running off the road at the safety points should the brakes be interfered with. (T. 67,953.)

7. **Creigiau Quarry Siding.**—This is a private siding, with facing points for Up trains. Trainmen must not proceed beyond the Gate until satisfied that the stop blocks have been unlocked and opened, and an "All Right" signal has been obtained from the Quarry Company's man.

8. Trainmen working at Creigiau Quarry must be careful before passing over the points to see that the Quarry Co.'s attendant is at the points, and that he has given an "All Right" signal. (A 54,148.)

9. Wagons for the Quarry must be delivered on to the loop clear of the Crossings, and the laden wagons must be placed by the Quarry Co. ready to be taken out without any shunting. (M. 34,853.)

10. **South Cambria.**—This is a Colliery siding, with facing points for Up trains ; empty wagons and goods traffic must be put off on the High Level or right hand sidings, and coal taken out from the Low Level or left hand siding.

11. **Torycoed.**—This is a Colliery siding, having two connections with the Single line, each of which is controlled from a ground frame unlocked by Annett's key, which accompanies the train staff for the Branch line. (5,737.)

12. The keys for the sidings upon this section are attached to the Train Staff for the section between Waterhall and Common Branch Junction.

Extracts from the Appendix to the TVR Working Timetable, 1913.

was authorised in February 1909. Pending completion of this siding, coal was loaded in the mileage siding, to the rear of Llantwit station goods yard. This siding had been authorised in October 1905, in response to complaints from Llantrisant and Llantwit Fardre Rural District Council over the lack of accommodation in the yard.

Another development in 1909 ushered in an enterprise of an altogether larger scale. On 13th October, 1909 a ceremony of cutting the first sod was held at the site of Cwm Colliery, near Beddau. A temporary siding was put in to facilitate development, this being superseded by a permanent arrangement in 1911. The colliery, owned by the Great Western Colliery Co., started production c. 1912, and was served by a private railway, 1¼ miles in length. At the junction with the main line, two connections were laid in, each controlled by a ground frame, with the ETS equipment housed in a central cabin. Cwm Colliery was a substantial undertaking by any standard and was to provide the mainstay of traffic on the Llantrisant branch for about 75 years.

Compared with the impressive scale of Cwm Colliery, Duffryn Llantwit Colliery, south-west of Llantwit station, was much more typical of the area. The siding was brought into use on 10th July, 1911, but did not last long, being taken up in 1920.

The development of these new sources of traffic was well-timed, following the closure of Glyn Colliery, which had closed, having been in receivership from at least February 1904.

This closure not only deprived the Treferig branch of most of its traffic, but also led to a falling away of traffic on Llantrisant No. 1 Railway, although this was later to return with the growth of output from Cwm Colliery.

Another new source of traffic was iron ore from the Llanharry Iron Ore Mine, which was connected to the Cowbridge branch in 1909. This was taken over the Llantrisant branch *en route* to Quakers Yard Junction, from where it was worked, via the steeply graded Taff Bargoed Joint Line, to Dowlais.

These developments were reflected in an increasing volume of freight traffic over the Llantrisant branch in the years up to World War I, even though it was to be some time before Cwm Colliery and Llanharry Iron Ore Mine were developed to their full extent. Goods train working was hampered by the long single line sections and heavy gradients. The maximum load permitted up the 1 in 40 banks, adjoining Llantrisant and Maesaraul Junctions, was only ten 10 ton loaded wagons, with 12 such wagons permitted on other severe gradients. At the foot of the former bank were sidings which served as the central point for the storage of cattle wagons on the TVR. Such wagons, returning from the GWR, via Llantrisant station, were first taken to Cowbridge for cleaning, before being worked to the storage sidings at Llantrisant Junction to await their next call to duty.

World War I brought with it a further increase in freight traffic, including large volumes of agricultural produce from Cowbridge and the Vale of Glamorgan. In addition, significant loads of timber were dispatched to aid the war effort. The extingencies of wartime also brought pressures for economies. In December 1916 the wartime Railway Executive Committee asked the TVR for details of any little-used lines that could be closed to provide permanent way materials to assist with the war effort. In reply, the TVR volunteered the closure of Llantrisant No. 1 Railway between Common Branch Junction and Creigiau Quarry (2 miles 2½ chains), the Llantrisant Common branch (2 miles 25 chains) and the Treferig branch (2 miles 58 chains), together with a number of other lines. The suggested closure of the Treferig branch brought forth protests from the Albion Coal Co. which was seeking to obtain stone for lining in its collieries from the district served by the branch. As a result, the TVR sought the deletion of this branch from the list of suggested closures. In the event, this proved unnecessary as in January 1917 the Railway Executive Committee decided that it did not require the permanent way materials from the lines in question.

The passenger train service was also a target for wartime economies. The first casualty came on 1st September, 1915, with the closure of Beddau Platform during the hours of darkness. From October 1917 the service was reduced to nine trains, each way, daily. More drastic cuts came in May 1918, when two more trains each way were withdrawn. This restricted timetable remained in force until May 1920, when the service was restored to its pre-war level of 10 trains, each way. All trains called at Beddau Platform from 1st January, 1920.

The return of peace focused attention on the future of the national railway system after the strain and lack of maintenance of the war years. Under the Railways Act of 19th August, 1921, the various independent companies of South Wales were amalgamated with the GWR. The TVR, the largest of the South Wales companies, was termed a 'constituent' rather than given the lesser status of an 'absorbed' company, and on 25th March, 1922 (but effective from 1st January of that year) it became part of the 'Greater' GWR.

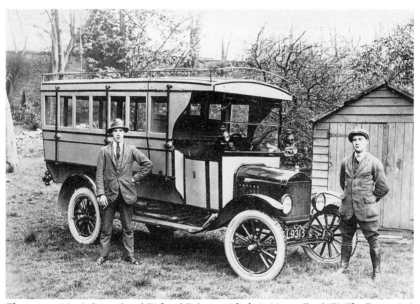

The competition! Samuel and Richard Palmer with their 14-seat Ford 'T' 'The Favourite' in June 1921.   *Pontypridd Library Collection*

Chapter Eight

Along the Lines

Pontypridd to Llantrisant

This description of the Llantrisant branches attempts to recreate the scene as it was in the last days of the TVR. Pontypridd station, the logical starting point for such a survey, was the hub of TVR passenger train services. Its unique layout, with three inset and two short motor bays, handled main line trains from Cardiff to Merthyr and Treherbert, together with branch line services radiating in all directions. Work on the new station, which replaced the earlier rather ramshackle affair, had commenced in 1907, but was not finally completed until 1914, although the new down main and 'PC&N Bay' platforms were brought into use on 7th March, 1910. The Llantrisant branch train, bound for Cowbridge and, somewhat less frequently, Aberthaw, departed from the latter platform. After leaving the confines of the station and rattling over the points at Pontypridd Caerphilly and Newport Junction, where the double track line, then the property of the Alexandra (Newport and South Wales) Docks and Railway Company, struck off to the left for Caerphilly, the train ran along the easternmost of the four tracks of the TVR main line to its first stop at Treforest. Here, the booking office on the down platform had been rebuilt after being gutted by fire on 18th March, 1908. Immediately after the station, the Barry Railway line to Tonteg Junction - later to be used by Llantrisant trains - departed to the right, while on the left were the remains of the short-lived connection to the Cardiff Railway.

At Llantrisant Junction, 2 miles 7 chains south of Pontypridd, the train slowed before crossing from the down main to the down relief line and passing on to the Llantrisant branch. The junction itself saw a number of changes over the years. Following the Board of Trade inspection in March 1865, its original layout of a trailing connection to the up line and trailing crossover was replaced by a conventional double line junction. In 1878 a down mineral line was added to the east of the running lines between Yniscoi and Treforest, passing through Llantrisant Junction, but without a facing connection to the down main line at the junction itself. A fourth line was added in 1885 when the arrangements were changed to provide up and down mineral lines to the west and up and down passenger lines to the east, with a double line connection between the two sets of lines. The mineral lines were upgraded to passenger standard in 1908. Llantrisant Junction was the scene of a major disaster on 12th August, 1893, when a Merthyr-Cardiff passenger train was derailed and 12 passengers killed.

Just after leaving the TVR main line, the Llantrisant branch had the appearance of a double track railway, as the running line was paralleled by a line leading to the cattle wagon storage sidings, located between the main and branch lines. An additional connection to these sidings went off at Llantrisant Junction South, where the small signal box had been replaced by a ground frame in 1894. The Llantrisant branch then began its 1 in 40 ascent out of the

The new station at Pontypridd, shortly after completion, with the vast island platform curving past the centre of the town. The mineral lines passed between the island platform and the cattle pens in the foreground. *Lens of Sutton*

'14XX' class 0-4-2T and auto-trailer in the bay at Pontypridd in 1949, having arrived from Llantrisant. *L&GRP*

The bay platform at Pontypridd, used by Llantrisant branch trains. *Mowat Collection*

Treforest station, looking towards Pontypridd, *c.* 1920. This was the last stop for Llantrisant branch trains before arriving at Pontypridd. In certain instances connections to and from Cardiff were made at Treforest, rather than Pontypridd. *B.J. Miller Collection*

An up empty excursion train just to the north of the site of Llantrisant Junction on the ex-TVR main line on 1st August, 1960.
S. Rickard

Llantrisant Junction signal box on the former TVR main line, with the S & T department at work alongside the box.
Welsh Industrial and Maritime Museum

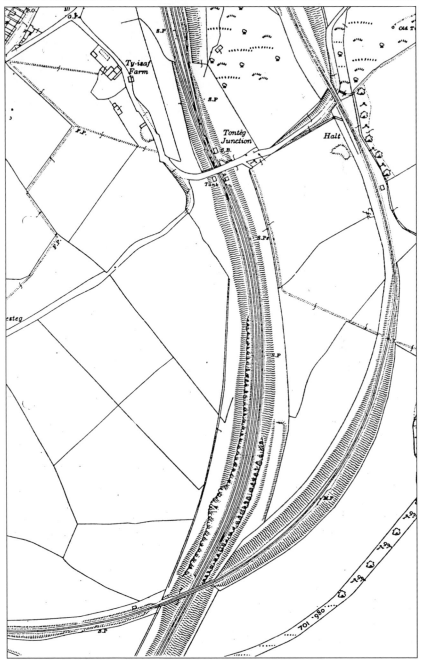

Tonteg Platform (TVR) on the single line, with Tonteg Junction on the nearby Barry Railway main line. *Reproduced from the 25″, 1915 Ordnance Survey Map*

The 11.52 am Cwm Colliery-Maritime minerals, hauled by '56XX' class 0-6-2T No. 5680, arrives at the junction with the former Barry Railway line from Tonteg Junction to Treforest on 25th October, 1956. The line on the left of the picture is the disused former Barry main line to Hafod Junction. *S. Rickard*

Tonteg Halt after the shelter had been removed from the Llantrisant branch platform. *D. Chaplin*

Taff valley on a ledge cut into the wooded hillside. At the top of the incline the train slowed to call at Tonteg Platform, which was reached by steps from the Tonteg-Upper Boat road, which passed under the railway at this point. Beyond Tonteg the line curved through a deep cutting to cross the Barry Railway main line, itself in a deeper cutting, by means of a girder bridge. Shortly after this bridge, the remains of Powell's Lantwit Vardre Railway merged with the Llantrisant branch from the left.

Approaching Church Village station, the train passed the site of Taff Llantwit Colliery sidings. The colliery itself had been situated about ¼ mile to the south, connected to the sidings by means of a tramway. Passing under a bridge carrying the Church Village-Efail Isaf road, built wide enough for double track, the train arrived at Church Village station, a single platform affair, with a brick-built station building surmounted by a large canopy. Original plans submitted to the Board of Trade in 1887 show a gabled structure and the canopy may have been added in 1898 as part of the alterations carried out at the station. In June 1913 the TVR rejected a request from Llantwit Fardre Parish Council that the station be renamed 'Tre Illtyd'. Just beyond the station, the train negotiated a sharp curve; to the north could be traced an even sharper curve which had been on the route of the Lantwit Vardre Railway.

From Church Village it was a relatively short run to Llantwit, the most important intermediate station on the Llantrisant branch. In its original form the station had comprised a single platform, with a red-brick station building and a goods siding serving a stone-built goods warehouse. A goods loop was later provided from which a short siding went off to serve the warehouse. In 1882 another loop was installed opposite the passenger station, in connection with the provision of a new connection to Garth Llantwit Colliery. This loop siding was equipped with a weighing machine and was accordingly known as the 'Machine Siding'. In 1885 material from the by then disused connection to Garth Llantwit Colliery was used to provide a short private siding off the Machine Siding to serve a small foundry opposite the passenger station. Under a agreement, dated 29th April, 1910, this siding was extended to form a loop off the old Machine Siding, serving the Llantwit Red Ash Colliery. The colliery itself, a typically small-scale affair, was situated to the north of Llantwit station, connected to the railway by a short section of tramway. The private siding agreement was later transferred to the British Red Ash Colliery Co. On 3rd June, 1917, whilst unloading an 18-ton boiler for this company, the TVR's 50-ton crane overbalanced and fell down the embankment. The foundry siding continued in use after the closure of the colliery. In 1946 the private siding agreement was transferred to the Nova Oil and Solvent Co. and was eventually terminated on 7th September, 1964. Beyond the station a private railway had originally left the main line to serve Tynant Colliery, but the line was later cut back to serve only Llest Llantwit Colliery, and connected to the goods loop. In 1909 this siding became the new Machine Siding, and in 1913 it was extended by 140 yards in the direction of Common Branch Junction.

Beyond Llantwit station the Llantrisant branch left the course of the Lantwit Vardre Railway, and the earthworks immediately took on a more substantial appearance. The line passed over an embankment and crossed a minor road by

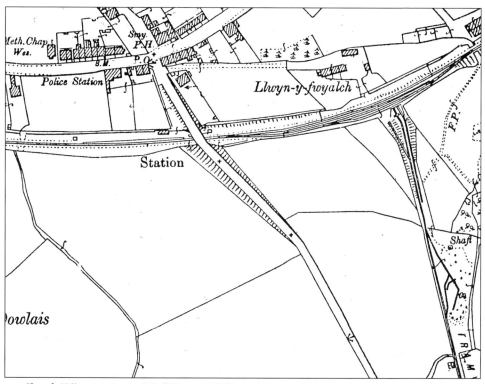

Church Village station and Taff Llantwit Colliery sidings and tramway.
Reproduced from the 25", 1898 Ordnance Survey Map

Church Village Halt, looking towards Pontypridd.   *Lens of Sutton*

means of a stone arched bridge. On the left were the remains of the sidings that had served Duffryn Llantwit Colliery. The line then passed through a deep cutting and under a footbridge to emerge at the junction with the Cwm Colliery private railway. There were two connections, trailing to down trains, forming a loop at the junction itself. In 1933 this loop was extended and the connections with the main line moved nearer to Common Branch Junction.

From Cwm Siding the railway ran across Gwaun Miskin Common on a low embankment to Beddau Platform. The platform itself was reached by steps from the adjoining minor road, which passed under the railway at this point, and stood on the site of Wallsend Colliery sidings. These had been lifted around the turn of the century and had been connected to the colliery by a single line tramway. Opposite the platform was a single traffic siding, added in 1878, and controlled, as were the colliery sidings, by a small signal cabin until 1894, when a ground frame was installed.

After Beddau Platform the railway passed through a cutting and under a bridge to Common Branch Junction, the hub of the former L&TVJR system. Here the Common branch left the main Llantrisant branch. It was also the junction for Llantrisant No. 1 Railway, although it was another ¼ mile before the two lines actually parted company. In the 'vee' between the Llantrisant branch and the Common branch were originally situated the engine shed and associated facilities, together with a carriage shed, but by the time of our journey all that remained were the sidings. Common Branch Junction signal cabin was a substantial timber-built structure, but was replaced, in GWR days, by a standard hipped-roof design. From this point, the Llantrisant No. 1 Railway ran parallel with the main Llantrisant branch to the site of Common Branch Junction West, where first the West Curve, and later the No. 1 Railway had joined the 'main line'. On 4th January, 1898 the TVR Traffic Committee accepted a recommendation to restore the west curve at Common Branch Junction, but, in the event, the new work was restricted to a dead-end siding off the Common branch, and the connection with the Llantrisant branch at the site of Common Branch Junction West was not restored.

From Common Branch Junction it was but a short run to Cross Inn station. The station served a small settlement, named after the local inn, and which in 1922 amounted to about 30 dwellings. Its real importance, however, lay in the fact that it was situated at the nearest point on the railway to the town of Llantrisant, about ⅓ mile to the west. The station occupied a very restricted site cut into the hillside, resulting in a very small and cramped layout. As opened on 6th September, 1869 Cross Inn station lacked goods facilities, but these were provided following a local petition, recorded by the *Cardiff Times* of 1st January, 1870. The diminutive goods yard comprised a short siding to a cattle pen, from where another siding ran back to serve a brick-built goods shed. Beyond Cross Inn the line continued its winding course to Maesaraul Junction, past Cottage Siding and the cottages which gave it its name. These had been built by the TVR in 1874, the siding, which augmented those at Cross Inn, being added in 1877. It was taken out of use in 1933. From Cottage Siding the line descended a 1 in 40 gradient to Maesaraul Junction. According to George Fisher, when giving evidence before the House of Commons Committee on the L&TVJR Bill in 1861,

Llantwit Fardre goods shed and station building from the approach road in 1954.

J. Hutton Collection

Llantwit Fardre station, looking towards Pontypridd, on 28th March, 1954, before track rationalisation took its toll.

H.C. Casserley

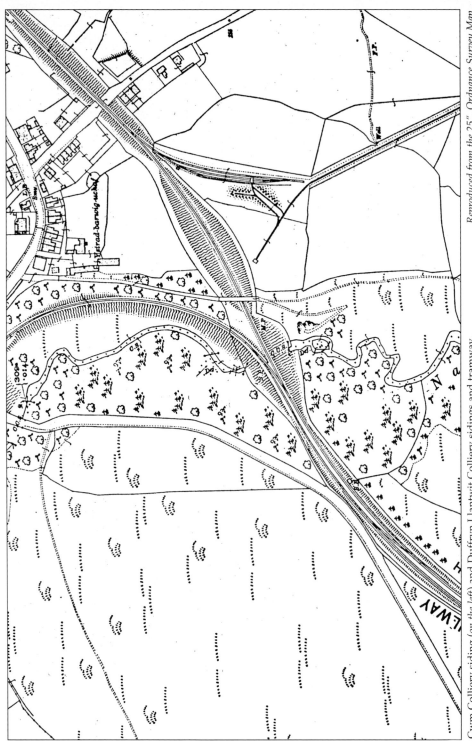

Cwm Colliery siding (*on the left*) and Duffryn Llantwit Colliery sidings and tramway.

Reproduced from the 25″, Ordnance Survey Map

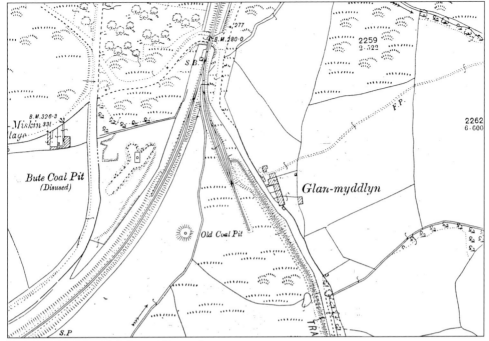

Llantwit Wallsend Colliery siding and tramway.

Reproduced from the 25", 1897 Ordnance Survey Map

Beddau Platform.

Reproduced from the 25", 1915 Ordnance Survey Map

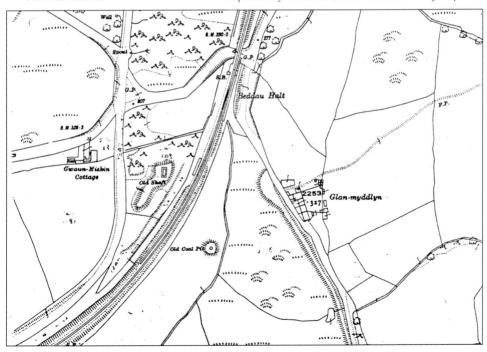

Common Branch Junction on 31st July, 1960. The line on the right of the picture is Llantrisant No. 1 Railway from Waterhall Junction, whilst that on the left is the main Llantrisant branch. Common Branch Junction engine shed was originally situated just to the left of the signal box.
M. Hale

A '56XX' class 0-6-2T waits for a clear road at Common Branch Junction on 9th November, 1951.
Welsh Industrial and Maritime Museum

Cross Inn station on 15th July, 1959, showing the goods shed after the yard sidings had been lifted. *R.M. Casserley*

Cross Inn station, looking towards Llantrisant, on 31st July, 1960. *M. Hale*

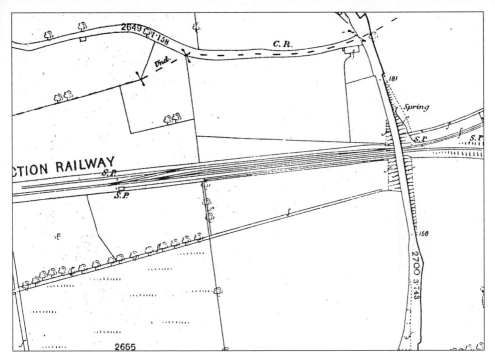

Maesaraul Junction.

Reproduced from the 25", 1875 Ordnance Survey Map

Maesaraul Junction.

Reproduced from the 25", 1915 Ordnance Survey Map

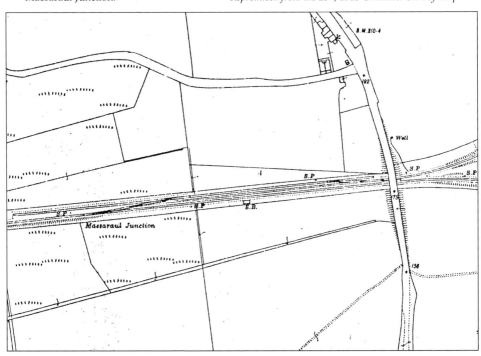

The parting of the ways at Maesaraul Junction on 24th May 1959, with the Llantrisant branch curving away on the left of the picture and the Mwyndy branch on the right. *M. Hale*

'57XX' class 0-6-0PT No. 5788 and '42XX' class 2-8-0T No. 4261 coast down the 1 in 40 incline to Maesaraul Junction, having worked from Cwm Colliery on 3rd May, 1958. *S. Rickard*

Maesaraul Junction, looking towards Llantrisant. *G. Croad Collection*

Maesaraul Junction, in its later simplified form, looking towards Cross Inn. *G. Croad Collection*

Llantrisant station looking towards Cardiff, just prior to World War I, with the TVR goods station on the extreme right of the picture. *Lens of Sutton*

Llantrisant Common Junction signal box on the Ely Valley line on 3rd June, 1965. This box had replaced an earlier one in 1924 and was itself closed on 3rd October, 1965. *M. Hale*

the layout of the railway at this point was expressly designed to facilitate an extension to Cowbridge: 'The termination of the line near the Mwyndy Branch is considerably above the valley with the express object of extending it further in the direction of Cowbridge and very good gradients could be obtained from there in that direction'. When the Cowbridge Company abandoned its intention to build a direct line to join the L&TVJR, the Llantrisant branch was left with an unnecessarily steep gradient, near Maesaraul Junction, which was to remain a constant source of operating difficulties.

At Maesaraul Junction the Llantrisant branch joined the Mwyndy branch of the GWR and, from there to Llantrisant station, the TVR enjoyed running powers originally granted to the Cowbridge Railway. The junction itself was a simple affair with a single line connection and a loop on the TVR line.

From Maesaraul Junction the railway ran in virtually a straight line to Cowbridge Road Crossing, where the double track section commenced. The crossing itself was controlled by a neat standard GWR brick-built signal box. A larger box in a similar style controlled Mwyndy Junction, where the Mwyndy branch joined the main Ely Valley line. Curving sharply past extensive sidings and the locomotive depot, the line reached the South Wales main line. Penygraig branch trains ran into the bay on the up side of Llantrisant station, but the TVR train crossed the South Wales main line to reach the Cowbridge bay on the down side. Here the train reversed to continue its journey into the bucolic heart of the Vale of Glamorgan.

The Common Branch

Shortly after leaving Common Branch Junction, the siding laid on the route of the old West Curve trailed in from the left, and almost immediately after this was the junction with the Gelynog branch. At one time, Gelynog Junction was fully signalled, with a ground frame of six levers being listed in 1896. After the removal of the private railway, which formed a continuation of the branch to Gelynog Colliery, the line was cut back to the gates which marked the limit of railway ownership.

Just beyond this junction, the Common branch entered the northern part of Llantrisant Common, and, passing under the Common Road Bridge, reached Treferig Junction. Glyn Colliery workmen's trains originally worked from Treferig Junction, where miners were picked up or set down. There was no platform and miners were faced with a lengthy trudge over a footpath across the Common to reach the nearest road to Llantrisant. Later on, the trains worked to and from the Common Road bridge, which was far more convenient for Llantrisant. The 1903 working timetable shows the evening trains (Saturdays excepted) and the Saturday afternoon trains running through to Common Road bridge, while the up morning train still ran from Treferig Junction.

Just beyond Treferig Junction, the Common branch crossed Glanmychydd viaduct, of three spans, one each for the old Llantrisant-Tonyrefail road, the Nant Mychydd and the remains of the short-lived Castellau branch of the EVR.

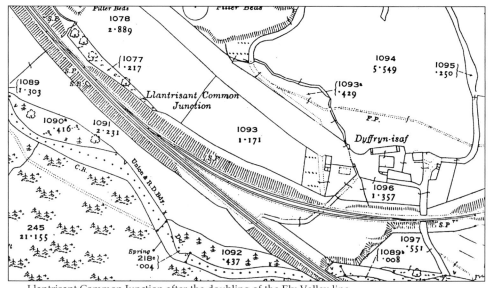

Llantrisant Common Junction after the doubling of the Ely Valley line.
Reproduced from the 25", 1914 Ordnance Survey Map

Glyn Colliery sidings at the terminus of the Treferig branch.
Reproduced from the 25", 1900 Ordnance Survey Map

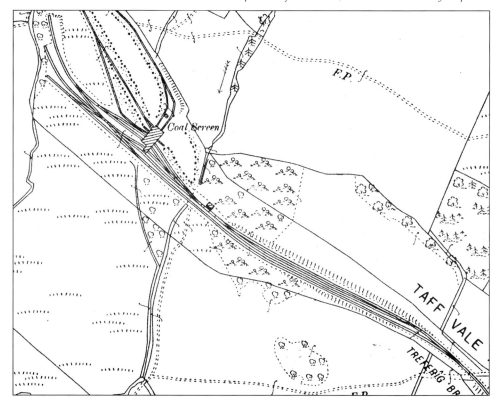

Beyond this viaduct, the line ran on a fairly substantial embankment before running into Llantrisant Common Junction, where it joined the Ely Valley branch of the GWR.

The Treferig Branch

Immediately beyond Treferig Junction was a loop siding, which had been used for stabling mineral trains *en route* to or from Glyn Colliery. Beyond this, the remains of the spur to the disused Castellau branch of the EVR merged with the Treferig branch from the left. This spur - Railway No. 1 of the Treferig Valley Railway Act of 1879 - had never been used for revenue traffic as the GWR had not relaid the old Castellau branch. Railway No. 1, had been disconnected from the main Treferig branch by 1897.

The Treferig branch followed a winding route up the unspoilt valley of the Nant Mychydd. After a short level section just beyond Treferig Junction, it was an uphill climb all the way to the terminus. As a result, mineral trains were always propelled up the branch.

After about a mile, the train reached Castellau Siding, a single mileage siding by a bridge carrying a minor road over the railway. The siding had been installed as a result of a request from the Agent of Aberpergwm Estate, in September 1897, for the benefit of nearby tenants, but it also served an adjoining saw mill. Castellau Siding, together with the earlier Treferig Siding further up the valley, had originally had trailing connections to the main line for trains working up the valley. Although this made sense in the event of a 'wild run' from further up the line, it necessitated the use of tow ropes in shunting operations, with the attendant dangers. The connections were altered to become facing for up trains, following an intervention by the Board of Trade in June 1903. In June 1906 the TVR Traffic Committee agreed to extend Castellau Siding to accommodate a chute for loading coal from nearby mining operations.

Beyond Castellau Siding, the line continued its winding and steeply graded course through attractive wooded countryside to Treferig (or Treferig Old Mill) Siding. In later years this was referred to as 'Treferig House Siding', the siding near Treferig Junction then being termed 'Treferig Siding'. Beyond this mileage siding the line was effectively disused after the closure of Glyn Colliery. At the colliery itself there were a number of loop sidings, one of which served the colliery screens, from where a tramway ran to the mine itself. The valley at this point opens out above Tonyrefail and its proximity to that settlement gave rise to a number of requests from the local Chamber of Trade for the Treferig branch to be extended to Tonyrefail, no doubt as a means of undermining the GWR's monopoly in this part of the Ely valley. There was no road access to Glyn Colliery, local miners making use of a footpath across the fields to Tonyrefail.

Former TVR distant signal, fixed at caution in GWR days, on Llantrisant No. 1 Railway, near Common Branch Junction on 15th February, 1958.

S. Rickard

The Llantrisant No. 1 Railway

After parting company with the Llantrisant branch at the site of Common Branch Junction West, the Llantrisant No. 1 Railway followed a twisting and in places switchback route through sparsely inhabited rolling countryside. At Torycoed Colliery, 78 chains from Common Branch Junction, a loop siding served the mine on the south side of the railway. All other sidings between Waterhall Junction loop and Common Branch Junction were facing to up trains (i.e., towards Common Branch Junction), which greatly aided shunting operations as all trains were propelled in this direction. After about 1½ miles of easier gradients, the branch passed under the Barry Railway main line, and shortly after, at 2 miles 36 chains, the siding from South Cambria Colliery trailed in from the left. From this point the No. 1 Railway ran parallel to the Barry line to a point opposite Creigiau station, where a siding went off to serve Creigiau Quarry. From here the branch turned away from the Barry line to continue its course to Waterhall Junction. Mileage sidings were provided at Pantygored (3 miles 6 chains) and St Fagans Road (5 miles 5 chains). The former was removed in April 1940, while the latter was not taken out of use until 4th March, 1962. Approaching Waterhall Junction, a loop siding provided a refuge for down traffic but could also be used to pass trains. Waterhall Junction itself was controlled by a stone-built signal box provided for the opening of Llantrisant No. 1 Railway in 1886.

The branch was worked by train staff and ticket, with the sidings controlled by ground frames unlocked by a key attached to the train staff.

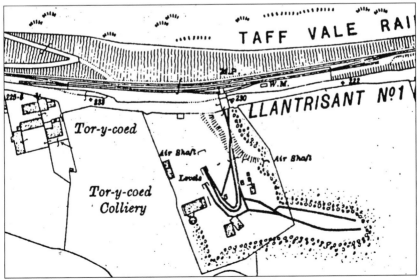

Tor-y-coed Colliery and sidings on Llantrisant No. 1 Railway.
Reproduced from the 25", 1915 Ordnance Survey Map

Waterhall Junction showing the unusual layout involving a trailing connection from Llantrisant No. 1 Railway to the down Penarth line, with a single slip providing a trailing connection between the up and down lines.
M. Hale

Waterhall Junction signal box. This box opened with Llantrisant No. 1 Railway in 1886.
D. Chaplin

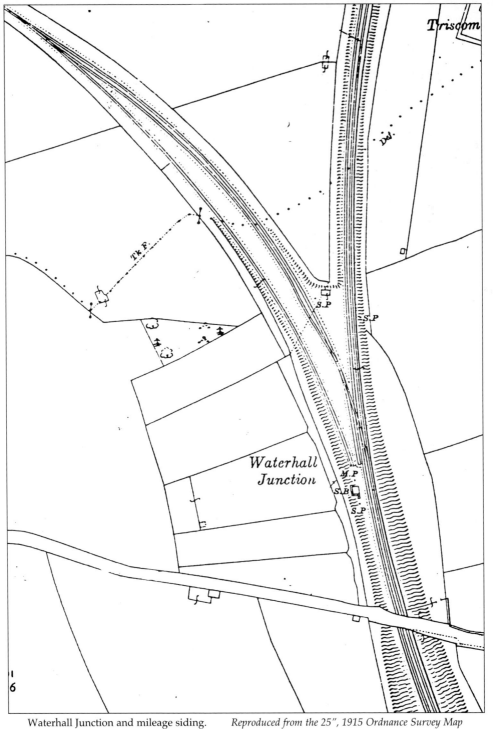

Waterhall Junction and mileage siding.   *Reproduced from the 25", 1915 Ordnance Survey Map*

PONTYPRIDD AND LLANTRISANT. (Week Days only.)

Down — SATURDAYS EXCEPTED

	a.m.	a.m.	p.m.	p.m.	p.m.	p.m.
Pontypridd (Central) dep.	7 0	10 0	1 33	4 34	5 13	8 30
Treforest (Low Level)	7 4	10 4	1 42	4 38	5 17	8 34
Tonteg Halt	7 12	10 12	1 50	4 44	5 24	8 41
Church Village	7 16	10 16	1 54	4 48	5 28	8 45
Llantwit	7 19	10 20	1 57	4 50	5 32	8 49
Beddau Halt	7 24	10 25	2 2	…	5 37	8 58
Cross Inn	7 30	10 30	2 8	…	5 45	9 0
Llantrisant arr.	7 35	10 38	2 13	4 59	5 50	9 5

Up — SATURDAYS EXCEPTED

	a.m.	a.m.	p.m.	p.m.	p.m.	p.m.
Llantrisant dep.	7 45	8 33	12 53	3 55	5 5	7 25
Cross Inn	7 53	8 41	1 5	4 8	5 9	7 32
Beddau Halt	8 3	8 47	1 9	4 13	5 13	7 39
Llantwit	8 7	8 52	1 13	4 17	5 15	7 43
Church Village	8 12	8 56	1 17	4 21	5 15	7 47
Tonteg Halt	8 15	9 1	1 18	4 27	…	7 51
Treforest (Low Level)	8 18	9 8	1 23	…	…	7 57
Pontypridd (Central) arr.	8 21	9 10	1 26	4 31	5 18	8 0

PONTYPRIDD AND LLANTRISANT. Rail Auto Car, one class only. (Week Days only.)

Down

Miles		a.m.	a.m.	a.m.	a.m.	p.m.	p.m.	p.m.	p.m.
—	Pontypridd dep.	7 4	8 33	10 0	11 47	12 56	1 41	…	…
1	Treforest	7 7	8 36	10 5	11 50	1 4	1 44	…	…
2¼	Tonteg Halt	7 13	8 42	10 13	11 56	1 10	1 50	…	…
4	Church Village	7 17	8 46	10 17	12 0	1 14	1 54	…	…
4½	Llantwit	7 20	8 49	10 20	12 3	1 17	1 57	…	…
6½	Beddau Halt	7 24	8 53	10 28	12 7	2 1	2 6	…	…
	Cross Inn	7 28	8 57	10 28	12 11	2 5	2 6	…	…
8½	Llantrisant arr.	7 33	9 2	10 33	12 16	2 14	2 14	…	…

Up — SATURDAYS EXCEPTED

	a.m.	a.m.	p.m.	p.m.	p.m.	p.m.	p.m.	p.m.
Llantrisant dep.	7 15	8 32	10 30	12 56	1 41	2 5	3 57	4 54
Cross Inn	7 22	8 39	10 37	1 2	1 4	2 12	4 4	4 57
Beddau Halt	7 30	8 43	10 41	1 6	1 6	2 16	4 8	4 45
Llantwit	7 34	8 51	10 45	1 10	1 11	2 20	4 12	4 47
Church Village	7 37	8 54	10 48	1 13	1 14	2 23	4 15	4 49
Tonteg Halt	7 41	8 58	10 52	1 17	1 18	2 27	4 19	…
Treforest	7 47	9 4	10 58	1 23	1 23	2 33	4 25	…
Pontypridd arr.	7 50	9 7	11 1	1 26	1 26	2 36	4 28	…

WATERHALL JUNCTION AND COMMON BRANCH JUNCTION. Single Line—Train Staff and Ticket.

Down Trains.

Distance from Common Br Jc. (M C)	STATIONS	Gradient 1 in	Time Allowance for Ordinary Freight Trains (Point to Point times)	Allow for stop.	9.45 a.m. Cwm Colliery Coal (arr)	(dep)	Dowlais Cardiff Works Goods (arr)	(dep)	3.32 p.m. Cwm Colliery Coal (dep)
—	Common Branch Junction	50R	…	…		9 55		p.m.		p.m.
0 78	Torpwood Colliery	58E	5	1		W		12 50		W
2 4	South Cambria Collieries	118F	5	1		W		W		W
2 36	Creigiau Quarries	137F	4	1						
3 6	Pantygored Siding	81F	3	1						
5 6	St. Fagans Road Siding	65R		2		10 25P	10 28	14 P	14 P	4 11
7 1	Waterhall Junction	111F	2			H2		Y16	1 17	H12

Up Trains. **Week Days only.**

Station No.	STATIONS	Gradient 1 in	Time Allowance for Ordinary Freight Trains (Point to Point Times)	Allow for start.	8.20 a.m. Pen'rth Curve Empties (dep)	10.55 a.m. Rarly Junction Goods (arr)	(dep)	1.50 p.m. Pen'rth Curve Empties (dep)
7707	Waterhall Junction	111R	10		a.m.	a.m. 11 28	11 35	p.m.
	St. Fagans Road Siding	65F	9	1	W	C	12	W
	Pantygored Siding	81R	4	1		11 53	12 9	
	Creigiau Quarries	137R	2	1			3	
	South Cambria Collieries	118R	5	1				
	Torpwood Colliery	68R	5	1				
	Common Branch Junction	50F			9 6			4 40
					H2	Y16		H12

Extracts from the GWR Public Timetable; (top) General Strike, 1926; (centre) 7th July-21st September, 1930; (bottom) September 1931.

Chapter Nine

Under the Great Western

By the time of the Grouping local railwaymen could feel able to put the pressures and uncertainties of the war years behind them and look forward, with reasonable confidence, to the future. Certainly, the main Llantrisant branch was relatively busy. The passenger timetable had been restored to its pre-war glory in 1920, with 10 trains each way. In 1923 just over 89,000 tickets were sold at stations along the line, the total being divided fairly evenly between the three stations, and representing a daily average of nearly 300 tickets, excluding seasons. There was also a substantial number of passengers from Llantrisant station, booked over the former TVR line. Freight traffic was also fairly buoyant, with the main branch generating nearly 250,000 tons in 1923, most of which was coal from Cwm Colliery. Creigiau Quarry, on Llantrisant No. 1 Railway, added to this with substantial quantities of stone. Through traffic was also important, being dominated by the flow of iron ore from Llanharry to Dowlais, by this time routed via the ex-TVR Nelson branch to Ffaldcaiach for the long drag up to the steel works. During the 1920s this traffic required the running of up to three loaded trains daily. Station staff at this time amounted to three at Church Village, eleven at Llantwit and ten at Cross Inn.

Evidence of the change of ownership brought about by the Grouping soon began to appear. Tonteg and Beddau Platforms soon acquired the more general title of 'Halt'. Other changes were equally cosmetic, with much of the old TVR character persisting for many years.

The 1920s saw the rapid development of bus services in the Llantrisant and Llantwit Fardre area, with at least 12 operators being present in 1925. There were two main routes: Pontypridd-Beddau and Pontypridd-Llantrisant and beyond. S.J. Palmer introduced the first service on the Beddau route in June 1921, while later that year South Wales Commercial Motors (SWCM) commenced a Pontypridd-Llantrisant-Bridgend service. While SWCM had the through route almost to itself for a number of years, there was intense competition on the Beddau route, where the buses were particularly attractive in view of the distance of the village from Beddau Halt. In June 1925, competition increased markedly with the arrival of the Rhondda Tramways Company, operating a Pontypridd-Llantrisant-Cowbridge service. The Rhondda Company's approach was highly combative, with aggressive fare-cutting and racing featuring strongly. In response, seven of the independent companies, S.A. Bebb of Llantwit Fardre, J.A. Cox of Treforest, D.J .& E. Gray of Tonteg, R. Maisey of Church Village and S.J. Palmer, joined forces to form 'Amalgamated Bus Services' (ABS). The companies remained independent, but shared a joint ticketing and timetabling arrangement under the 'ABS' name. After a period of manic competition, things settled down somewhat, with ABS concentrating on the Beddau route and Rhondda and SWCM sharing the Llantrisant route. In 1929 SWCM became a major part of the Western Welsh

Omnibus Company.

This degree of competition had a catastrophic impact on the passenger business of the Llantrisant branch. The relatively short distances, coupled with the linear form of much of the settlement pattern, favoured bus operation at the expense of rail. When frequency and fare levels were taken into account, it was clear that the railway was at a considerable disadvantage. The resulting decline in patronage is apparent in the reduction in ticket sales at branch stations, with the total sold down from nearly 90,000 in 1923, to under 12,000 in 1931. Church Village and Llantwit stations were especially vulnerable, with ticket sales in 1931 being only ten and six per cent respectively of the 1923 levels. Cross Inn fared slightly better with its 1931 total amounting to 20 per cent of that in 1923. This decline was not matched by any significant operating economies. Some reductions were made in staffing, with Church Village reduced to the status of an unstaffed halt on 14th March, 1932, but the passenger service remained at 10 trains each way, Mondays to Saturdays. With the end of through working to and from Cowbridge, Llantrisant branch trains were able to make use of the Penygraig bay at Llantrisant station, thereby avoiding the need to cross the South Wales main line, with the potential for delays that entailed.

Freight traffic over the Llantrisant branches experienced mixed fortunes during the 1920s, with coal traffic declining from a high point in 1923. Potentially devastating was the closure of Cwm Colliery in 1927. As a result, the two coal workings over Llantrisant No. 1 Railway were withdrawn, leaving only a single stone working between Creigiau and Waterhall Junction. This closure proved only temporary, however, as the Colliery re-opened in 1929, after which production grew substantially, reaching over 400,000 tons per annum in 1933. In 1936 the private siding agreement was transferred to the Powell Duffryn Associated Collieries Co., thereby restoring the Powell name to the Llantwit Fardre coalfield. The rebirth of Cwm provided the exception, however, and apart from this the 1920s were years of contraction for the local coal industry. Duffryn Llantwit Colliery siding had been taken up in 1920. Torycoed was taken out of use in 1926, although it was to re-open under the Cymric Colliery Co. between 1930 and 1934. The private siding agreement for South Glamorgan Colliery, on Llantrisant No. 1 Railway, was terminated on 1st February, 1928. Though iron ore traffic continued at a high level throughout the 1920s, but ceased with the end of steel making at Dowlais in 1930.

The Grouping provided an opportunity for the identification and elimination of duplicate and redundant facilities. The Treferig branch, virtually disused above Treferig House Siding since the closure of Glyn Colliery, was an early target, with the section between Glyn Colliery and Treferig House Siding being removed in October 1928, followed by that above Castellau Siding, in October 1933. The Common branch was closed as a through route in 1930/31, with the middle section being removed in late 1931. The line between Common Branch Junction and Castellau Siding remained in use to serve a sawmill, but this too was closed on 24th October, 1935, track being removed between April and August 1936. This left only a short section of the Common branch at the Llantrisant Common Junction end, which remained in use for wagon storage, until it too was closed on 1st July, 1951.

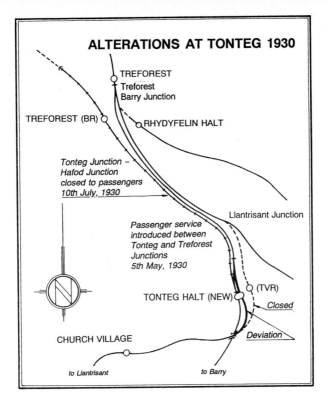

ALTERATIONS AT TONTEG 1930

TREFOREST

Treforest
Barry Junction

TREFOREST (BR)

RHYDYFELIN HALT

*Tonteg Junction –
Hafod Junction
closed to passengers
10th July, 1930*

Llantrisant Junction

*Passenger service
introduced between
Tonteg and Treforest
Junctions
5th May, 1930*

TONTEG HALT (NEW)

(TVR)

Closed

CHURCH VILLAGE

Deviation

to Llantrisant

to Barry

Ex-TVR class 'A' 0-6-2T No. 397 with two ex-TVR coaches (converted from steam motor cars) climbs away from Tonteg Halt on a Llantrisant working on 5th June, 1948.   *I.L. Wright*

Rationalisation also took place at Maesaraul Junction; on 26th July, 1929, the GWR Traffic Committee ordered the abolition of the signal box and the removal of all signalling. Henceforth, the junction was controlled by a ground frame unlocked by the train staff for the section of line between Cowbridge Road Crossing (on the ex-EVR Mwyndy branch) and Common Branch Junction. The junction itself was relocated, on 20th May, 1945, to a point beneath the bridge carrying the Llantrisant-Miskin road.

A much more extensive rationalisation scheme was that completed in the Treforest area in 1930. Under its Act of 26th July, 1929 the GWR obtained powers to build a new connecting line between the former Barry and TVR lines at Tonteg. This enabled the steeply graded section of the Llantrisant branch down to Llantrisant Junction to be taken out of use. Tonteg Halt was replaced by a new halt at the junction with the Barry line. The new line was connected to the Llantrisant branch on Sunday 4th May, 1930, and was brought into use, together with the new Tonteg Halt, the following day. Llantrisant trains then ran via the upgraded section of the former Barry Railway from Tonteg Junction to the ex-TVR Main line at Treforest. They were joined by Barry line trains on 10th July, 1930, following the closure of the Tonteg Junction-Trehafod section to passenger traffic.

It was not until 21st March, 1932 that the new arrangements were inspected for the Ministry of Transport. In his report Lt Col A.H.L. Mount noted that the following alterations had been carried out:

At Tonteg, a single line loop connection, 31 chains long, has been constructed to provide direct access, over a gradient of 1 in 69, to and from the Taff Vale-Llantrisant Branch, thus eliminating the portion of steeply graded single line (1 in 40) to the existing junction of this branch with the main line at Maesmawr, lower down the valley.

The line is constructed on a curve of 10½ chains radius, and is in cutting (glacial drift) some 20 feet deep at a maximum. The rails weigh 95 1b per yard, are 45 feet long and are laid in 46 1b chairs on creosoted sleepers of standard size and spacing. Fencing is adequate and drainage arrangements in the cutting appear to be satisfactory.

Three halt platforms have been provided at Tonteg, namely one on the new single line connection, and on the up and down sides of the Barry Section. These platforms are 125 feet long, formed of massed concrete walling, are ash filled and surfaced with gravel. They are electrically lighted and access is obtained from the adjacent road overbridge, as shown on the plan, special arrangements having been made for milk traffic. There is shelter on each platform. Tonteg box has a new frame of 36 working levers and 10 spaces, including 2 detonator placers, the old locking having been reproduced. So far as time permitted, the additional locking in connection with the new single line junction was tested and found correct, and the signalman had no remarks to offer.

The existing line from Tonteg to Treforest 1¾. miles long, the gradient of which falls at 1 in 101, has been relaid with second hand rails weighing not less than 86 lbs per yard, on new sleepers and ballast.

At Maesmawr (Taff Vale) the junction with the Llantrisant Branch, and the portion of this branch which runs up the hillside, have been removed, as already mentioned, and a rearrangement of the running lines and sidings has been effected . . .

Mount went on to note that Llantrisant Junction and Maesmawr signal boxes had been replaced by a new central box, also called Maesmawr, containing 54

'64XX' class 0-6-0PT and auto-trailer near Llantwit Fardre station on 25th April, 1946.
I.L. Wright

'Metro' class 2-4-0T No. 3594 coupled to auto-trailer No. 106 on a Llantrisant branch working at Pontypridd on 14th August, 1946. *I.L. Wright*

Ex-TVR class 'A' 0-6-2T No. 304 leaves Church Village for Pontypridd on 7th May, 1948, past the site of Taff Llantwit Colliery Siding. *I.L. Wright*

'Metro' class 2-4-0T No. 3586 speeds a Llantrisant to Pontypridd working, near Common Branch Junction, on 5th June, 1948. *I.L. Wright*

working and 11 spare levers. He was perfectly satisfied with the arrangements and recommended that final approval be given.

Llantwit station was renamed 'Llantwit Fardre' on 8th October, 1936, presumably to distinguish it from Llantwit Major on the Vale of Glamorgan line.

Passenger traffic continued at a very low level throughout the 1930s. With the introduction of the wartime emergency timetable on 25th September, 1939, the service was cut from ten to six trains, each way. Traffic picked up, however, with the imposition of petrol rationing. One particular development produced hitherto unheard of levels of traffic for the Llantrisant branch. In 1939 platforms had opened at Tremains, just outside Bridgend, to serve a Royal Ordnance Factory. This was served by special trains from various places throughout South Wales. Three of these, from Treherbert, Maerdy and Merthyr, worked over the Llantrisant branch, running three times each way, in connection with the factory shift system, and usually arriving at Llantrisant within minutes of each other.

With the coming of peace and the ending of petrol rationing, traffic soon returned to its dismal pre-war levels. On 1st January, 1948 the Llantrisant branches became part of the nationalised British Railways.

A wartime view of Church Village Halt, looking towards Llantwit Fardre.   *J. Burrell*

The site of Tonteg Platform (TVR) on 6th April, 1958.

M. Hale

A coke train from Cwm Colliery, hauled by a '56XX' class 0-6-2T, coasts down the incline into Tonteg Halt.

D. Chaplin

Chapter Ten

Decline and Fall

Nationalisation did not bring any immediate or dramatic changes to the Llantrisant branches; for a time things continued much as before. By 1951, however, the passenger service was virtually moribund and was reduced to only four trains, each way, with an additional round trip on Saturdays. The average load was reported to be only five or six passengers at a time when the competing bus service, jointly worked by the Western Welsh and Rhondda companies, was operating at a half-hourly frequency. With no prospect of an upturn in the railway's fortunes, consultations took place with Llantrisant and Llantwit Fardre Rural District Council, Pontypridd Urban District Council and the railway unions with a view to withdrawing the passenger train service. There does not appear to have been any opposition to this proposal, and the date of withdrawal was fixed for Monday 31st March, 1952. The last day of service, Saturday 29th March, saw the usual influx of passengers and variety of motives associated with such occasions. At 9.55 pm, in snowy conditions, the last train, appropriately formed by an ex-TVR auto-set, pulled out of Pontypridd, watched by a small crowd of railway workers, enthusiasts and members of the public. The locomotive was driven by J. Priest, with fireman H. Blanch and the guard W.T. Gardiner. Following the withdrawal of the passenger train service, all stations and halts between Treforest and Llantrisant were closed to passengers, with the exception of Tonteg Halt, where the Barry line platforms remained in use until the withdrawal of Pontypridd to Barry and Cardiff, via St Fagans, services on 10th September, 1962.

Summer excursions from Pontypridd and valleys stations to Porthcawl continued to work over the Llantrisant branch after the withdrawal of the passenger train service. In the down direction (i.e., towards Porthcawl) such trains ran into the former Cowbridge branch bay for reversal, before continuing their journey, via the South Wales main line. Porthcawl excursions ceased to run over the Llantrisant branch after the 1959 season.

Freight traffic received a significant boost as a result of major re-investment at Cwm Colliery in the early 1950s. In conjunction with this work, the railway connection was radically altered, with the old winding route of the private railway being replaced by a virtually straight run from the Llantrisant branch to the colliery. The new junction with the main line, about ¼ mile nearer Common Branch Junction, was brought into use on 27th September, 1953.

Change of a more depressing, but soon to become more typical kind occurred in 1957, with a substantial reduction of facilities at Llantwit Fardre station. On 11th June, 1957 Llantwit Fardre signal box was abolished, the passing loop being converted into a loop siding, controlled by two ground frames. At the same time the former Machine Siding, opposite the station platform, was lifted, together with the mileage siding in the goods yard. By this time local goods traffic on the Llantrisant branches had declined to a very low level. Cross Inn yard had been taken out of use on 30th August, 1953. St Fagans Road Siding on

'64XX' class 0-6-0PT No. 6423 propels two ex-TVR auto-trailers on an SLS special at St Fagans Road Siding on Llantrisant No. 1 Railway on 12th July, 1952. The train reversed at Common Branch Junction and ran down to Llantrisant. Later in the day it worked over the full length of the Llantrisant branch *en route* to Pontypridd and Cilfynydd.   *S. Rickard*

A '56XX' class 0-6-2T No. 5699 arrives at Tonteg Halt on the 11.00 am Llantrisant-Coke Ovens mixed goods on 25th October, 1956.   *S. Rickard*

Llantrisant, looking west from the Cowbridge bay on 15th July, 1959, with the remains of the TVR goods station on the left of the picture. *H. C. Casserley*

Church Village Halt following withdrawal of passenger service and conversion of the station building to commercial use, 21st July, 1960. *M. Hale*

'The Leek', an excursion train jointly organised by the Monmouthshire Railway Society and the West Glamorgan Railway Society at Llantrisant on 27th June, 1964. This train ran over the Llantrisant branch from Pontypridd and was the last passenger working over the section between Tonteg Junction and Cwm Colliery Siding. *Westrail Enterprise*

Llantrisant station in 1965, after the withdrawal of the main line stopping trains, and showing the modified connection to the Cowbridge bay from the down main line. *Lens of Sutton*

Llantrisant No. 1 Railway went on 4th March, 1962 whilst Llantwit Fardre finally closed on 7th October, 1963. The mileage siding at Waterhall Junction lasted a little longer, until 13th July, 1964.

This was but a foretaste of what was to come. By 1964 there were only two sources of traffic on Llantrisant branches: Cwm Colliery on the Llantrisant branch itself and Creigiau Quarry on Llantrisant No. 1 Railway. Traditionally, Cwm Colliery had been served from the Treforest end of the Llantrisant branch, while Creigiau Quarry traffic had been worked, via Waterhall Junction, from Radyr. A single coal train from Cwm Colliery had worked over Llantrisant No. 1 Railway, but this had been withdrawn, leaving the Common Branch Junction-Creigiau section without traffic, and resulting in its closure from 17th June, 1963. In the wake of the Beeching Report in 1963 a complete reorganisation of the local railway network was proposed, with the working of coal traffic from Cwm Colliery and the Ely valley, stone from Creigiau Quarry and iron ore from Llanharry concentrated at Llantrisant. Closure of the Cwm Colliery-Treforest section was originally scheduled for 6th April, 1964, but was postponed at the last minute. The various changes associated with this reorganisation took place on 28th September, 1964: the lines from Cwm Colliery siding to Treforest and from Creigiau Quarry to Waterhall Junction were closed; the section from Common Branch Junction to Creigiau Quarry was reinstated; Common Branch Junction signal box was abolished and the branches beyond Cowbridge Road Crossing signal box worked as sidings. Tonteg Junction signal box lingered on until the following day. At Waterhall Junction the branch line was taken out on 26th October, 1964, but the signal box remained in use until 12th December, 1965. Track removal on the closed sections of line was completed in January 1966.

The closure of the Cwm Siding-Treforest Junction section was preceded, on 27th June, 1964 by the passing of a final enthusiasts' excursion, bearing the headboard 'The Leek'. This train, jointly organised by West Glamorgan Railway Society and the Monmouthshire Railway Society, was formed by a six-coach suburban set hauled by '56XX' class 0-6-2T No. 6614. Starting from Cardiff, its route took it over several doomed branches, via Park Junction, near Newport, Machen, Caerphilly and Pontypridd, before running over the branch to Llantrisant. It reversed in the Cowbridge branch bay, before continuing down that branch as far as Cowbridge Junction. After its return to Llantrisant, it made its way back to Cardiff via Bridgend and the Vale of Glamorgan line.

Other local casualties of this period of retrenchment included Llantrisant station, closed to passengers on 2nd November, 1964, and having lost its other branch services to Cowbridge on 26th November, 1951 and to Penygraig on 9th June, 1958. The goods service from Llantrisant to Cowbridge was withdrawn on 1st February, 1965, with that branch being cut back to Llanharry Iron Ore Mine. This was followed, on 7th October, 1968, by the closure of the remains of Broviskin branch, from Maesaraul Junction to an ICI gunpowder depot at Mwyndy.

The truncated remains of the Llantrisant branches, resulting from the closures of 1964, survived intact for nearly 15 years before further reduction took place. Llanharry Iron Ore Mine had closed on 25th July, 1975, leaving the stone traffic from Creigiau to be worked alone to East Moors Steelworks. The last revenue train, consisting of just two 35-ton hopper wagons with a brake van at each end

The rolling countryside through which the Llantrisant No. 1 Railway passed is well-illustrated in this view of a '94XX' class 0-6-0PT on a Creigiau Quarry to Radyr stone train.

Revd R.W.A. Jones

A stone train from Creigiau Quarry comes off Llantrisant No. 1 Railway at Waterhall Junction.

Revd R.W.A. Jones

Creigiau Quarry Sidings, June 1973. *R.W. Ranson*

Loaded and empty stone wagons at Creigiau Quarry Sidings, June 1973. *R.W. Ranson*

A class '37' Co-Co, working the 14.30 Llantrisant-Cwm Colliery empties, pauses at Cowbridge Road Crossing signal box on the former EVR section between Mwyndy Junction and Maesaraul Junction to accept the single line token on 17th June, 1982. *R.W. Ranson*

The 14.30 Llantrisant-Cwm Colliery empties, powered by class '37' Co-Co No. 37 270, arrives at the colliery sidings. *R.W. Ranson*

for reversal at Common Branch Junction, left Creigiau Quarry Siding on 30th September, 1977, hauled by a class '37' Co-Co No. 37 210. The Creigiau branch was closed to all traffic on 31st January, 1978, although it was not formally taken out of use until 1st January, 1981, there being some hope that stone traffic might revive. Indeed, this hope was sufficient to justify the running of a weed-killing train over the branch on 27th May, 1980. The hoped-for revival failed to materialise, however, and on 31st December, 1980 the siding agreement with British Steel was terminated. Track lifting proceeded from the Creigiau end, being undertaken by hand and road vehicle, although the Llantrisant pilot, a Class '08' 0-6-0 shunter, made several trips over the branch to drag back inaccessible lengths of rail. Dismantling was completed by March 1981.

The closure of the Creigiau branch heralded a new round of contraction in the railway network around Llantrisant. In September 1983 the residual goods facilities at Llantrisant, catering mainly for domestic coal, were withdrawn. Traffic over the remains of the Ely valley line ceased with the closure of Coed Ely coking plant, the terminus since the closure of the remainder of the branch on 2nd April, 1967. The last train, comprising class '08' No. 08 350 and five wagons, ran from Coed Ely on 4th October, 1983. A final excursion, formed of a 6-car class '117' dmu, ran over the line on 31st March, 1984, the line finally being taken out of use on 2nd April, 1984. On the Cwm Colliery section traffic remained sufficient to justify up to five return workings, Mondays to Fridays. On 10th October, 1983 Cowbridge Road Crossing signal box, on the former EVR section of the branch, was abolished, leaving the lifting barriers, which had been installed on 3rd February, 1974, to be operated by the train crew. At the same time, class '6' train working was introduced, thereby avoiding the need for brake vans on Cwm branch trains.

With the end of the national coal strike in March 1985, the final rundown of the South Wales Coalfield began in earnest. On 13th October, 1986 British Coal announced its intention to close Cwm Colliery. The last coal train left Cwm for Newport Docks on 2nd March, 1987, formed by class '37' No. 37 244 and 17 wagons. To mark the end of the branch an enthusiasts' excursion was organised by the Monmouthshire Railway Society. This train consisting of a two-car and a three-car dmu set, left Newport on Saturday, 11th April, 1987, and after running to Cwm and back to Cardiff, toured the Ferry Road, Tower Colliery, Ynysybwl and Nantgarw branches.

Llantrisant-Cwm Colliery
Working Timetable May 1982

Mondays to Fridays

Turn No.		1002	1002	1002	1003	1003
Description		Empties	Empties	Empties	Empties	Empties
Llantrisant	dep.	06.28	09.30	11.29	14.30	17.30
Cwm Colliery	arr.	06.46	09.48	11.47	14.48	17.48
Turn No.		1002	1002	1002	1003	1003
Description		Coal	Coal	Coal	Coal	Coal
Cwm Colliery	dep.	07.20	10.22	12.21	15.38	18.38
Llantrisant	arr.	07.58	11.00	12.59	16.16	19.16

Locomotive English Electric class '37' Co-Co.

TVR 2-4-0 No. 22, built Cardiff 1863/64.   *C. Chapman Collection*

TVR 0-4-4T No. 4, converted from 'Standard Goods' 0-6-0 No. 4 (built Cardiff, 1861, as *Dinas*). It was transferred to surplus stock in 1891 and withdrawn in February 1903.

M.E.M. Lloyd Collection

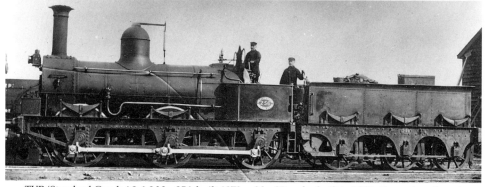

TVR 'Standard Goods' 0-6-0 No. 256, built 1870 as No. 28 and rebuilt in 1887. It was transferred to surplus stock in 1897 and withdrawn in 1899.   *P.J. Korrison Collection*

Chapter Eleven

Locomotive and Train Working

A full account of the locomotive history of the Taff Vale Railway may be found in Part 10 of *Locomotives of the Great Western Railway* published by the Railway Correspondence and Travel Society. It is not, therefore, necessary to cover the same ground in this study. The intention here is to record the types of locomotives and working arrangements found on the Llantrisant branches over the years.

Traffic over Thomas Powell's Lantwit Vardre Railway was worked by horses, apart from a short period when a locomotive was used. About May 1842 Powell acquired an engine which he hoped to use over the TVR, and on 30th June, 1842 he sought the permission of its Directors to do so. His request was met with outright opposition, the Board being of the opinion 'that it would be highly dangerous and inexpedient for other parties than the Company to work engines on the road'. Powell then made use of his engine, appropriately named *Llantwit*, on his Lantwit Vardre Railway for a time before reverting to horse power. In June 1844 the TVR agreed to Powell's application for the hire of wagons to bring down coal from Dihewyd Colliery. A further request, for 50 wagons, was made in the following September, Powell offering the TVR the use of *Llantwit* in return. This arrangement was followed, in December 1845, by the outright purchase by the TVR of *Llantwit* for £580. *Llantwit* was of C. & J. Rennie's build with 12 in. by 18 in. cylinders, suggesting an engine of 1838 vintage. Surviving TVR records describe *Llantwit* as a six-wheeled four-coupled locomotive with 4 ft 6 in. diameter driving wheels, and it would appear that she spent most of her days in TVR ownership working coal traffic on the company's Llancaiach branch. *Llantwit* was condemned in 1858.

A single locomotive, probably of the 'Standard Goods' 0-6-0 tender type, sufficed for L&TVJR traffic in the years immediately after its opening. Another engine was hired to the Cowbridge Railway and shedded at Cowbridge. After the introduction of the Cowbridge-Llantrisant-Pontypridd passenger service on 18th September, 1865, this engine worked two passenger trains each way over the L&TVJR, together with two goods workings over the Mwyndy branch of the EVR as far as Maesaraul Junction. The L&TVJR engine worked the remainder of the Mwyndy branch from Maesaraul Junction, where traffic was exchanged with the Cowbridge train.

The Cowbridge Company's decision in February 1870 to work its own traffic left the TVR without any facilities for locomotives working the passenger service over the L&TVJR. On 25th March, 1870 authority was given to erect a new engine shed at Maesaraul Junction. In the event, the shed was actually built at Common Branch Junction. It was opened later in 1870 and comprised a two road shed, together with coaling and watering facilities. There was also a carriage shed in which was stabled the stock for the Llantrisant-Pontypridd service, this being worked empty to and from Llantrisant at the beginning and end of each day's service. The service itself consisted of three round trips, with

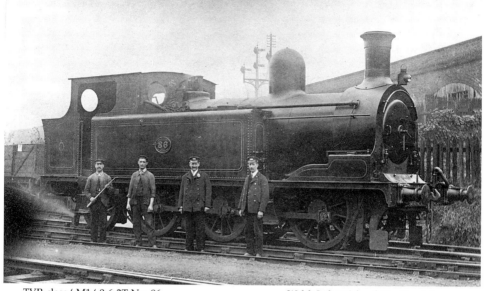

TVR class ' M1 ' 0-6-2T No. 86.

Welsh Industrial and Maritime Museum

TVR class 'K' 0-6-0 No. 3, built by Kitsons in 1881, photographed at Cardiff Cathays on 28th July, 1905.

LCGB

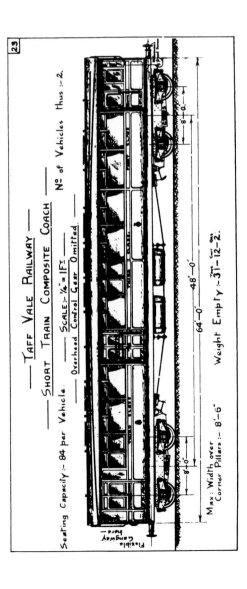

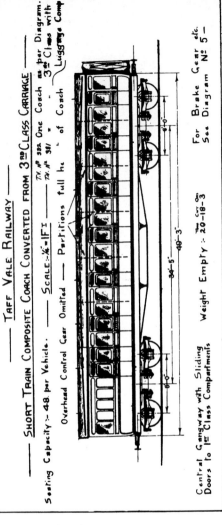

TVR diagram of 1st/3rd class auto-trailer (Nos. 78, 79) built by Bristol Wagon & Carriage Co. 1907.

TVR diagram of auto-trailer converted from 3rd class bogie carriage (Nos. 331, 332) built at Cathays in 1903 and converted in 1910.

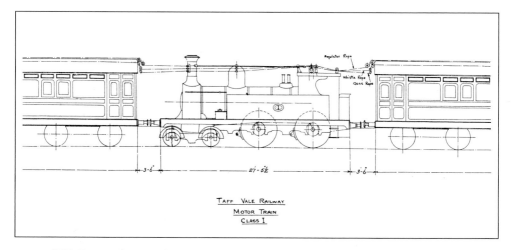

TVR diagram showing class 'I' 4-4-0T between two auto-trailers.

TVR locomotive unit for small motor car.

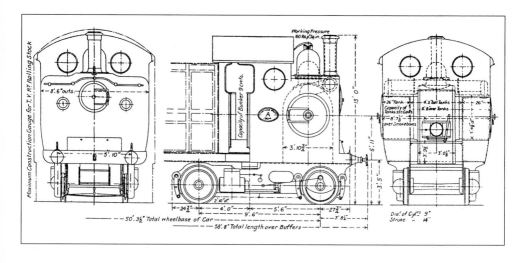

connections being made with certain Cowbridge trains at Llantrisant. Exchange of traffic between the two companies' goods trains continued to be made at Maesaraul Junction.

Through working between Cowbridge and Pontypridd was restored in 1875; following the leasing of the Cowbridge Railway by the TVR. As a result, the stabling of passenger engines at Common Branch Junction ceased, although the shed remained in use for goods and mineral engines. Little is known regarding the types of locomotive used at this time on the Llantrisant branch passenger train service, although it seems likely that early 2-4-0 tender engines were used, judging from E.L. Ahron's remark that 'on the appearance of the "No. 33" class (the last 2-4-0s introduced 1875-78) a few of their diminutive predecessors migrated to some of the branch lines'. In July 1875 the TVR Locomotive Engineer was instructed to convert an 0-6-0 tender engine of 1861 into an 0-4-4 tank engine for use on the Ferndale branch passenger service. Three more engines were similarly altered between 1878 and 1883. With the arrival of more powerful passenger tank engines from 1884, these engines (later 'J' class) gravitated to the Llantrisant and Cowbridge branches, being recorded by E.L. Ahrons, who noted that 'when I first saw them in 1887 most of the class were working between Pontypridd and Llantrisant, and also thence to Cowbridge'. The class became redundant with the appearance of large numbers of mixed traffic 0-6-2Ts in the 1890s. In 1884 and 1885 the TVR introduced three 4-4-0 tank engines, the later 'I' class. For a while they worked the main Cardiff to Merthyr and Treherbert services, but were later relegated to secondary duties, including the Llantrisant and Cowbridge services.

Goods and minerals trains at this time were worked by early 'Standard' class 0-6-0 tender engines, of which 44 had been built between 1859 and 1872. No. 56 of this type, dating from 1865, was involved in an accident at Llantwit on 5th July, 1884, when four wagons ran wild down the incline to Garth Llantwit Colliery, badly damaging five wagons. Details of train working in 1887 have survived which show that, at that time, passenger engines were shedded at Cowbridge, with goods and minerals workings shared by Common Branch Junction and Cardiff engines. Goods and minerals trains from Maesaraul Junction, Llantrisant Junction and Llantrisant No. 1 Railway all terminated at Llantwit station, where exchange of traffic took place.

On 10th May, 1890 instructions were given to provide water purifying equipment at Common Branch Junction shed. The following March the Locomotive Engineer reported that the engine shed was in need of rebuilding, and the water tank required renewal. A decision on this matter was repeatedly deferred, and the work does not appear to have been carried out. The locomotive allocation at Common Branch Junction had gone by 1897, although the shed remained in use for servicing for some time after this. It had been demolished by 1914, the nearby carriage shed having gone by 1894. Locomotives from a new steam shed at Coke Ovens, near Pontypridd, appeared following the opening of that shed in 1896.

In 1885 the TVR introduced the first engine of a type which was to become synonymous not just with that company, but with the railways of South Wales generally. The 'M' class 0-6-2T engines began to appear on the Llantrisant

TVR class 'O1' 0-6-2T No. 78.   *C. Chapman Collection*

TVR Motor Car No. 11, built Kerr, Stuart & Co. Ltd, at Cardiff Cathays.   *LCGB*

TVR class 'C' 4-4-2T No. 174 fitted with the TVR's somewhat unsightly style of auto-gear.

G.H.W. Clifford (Courtesy C.C. Green)

Former TVR class 'M1' 0-6-2T (No. 179) as GWR No . 491 and retaining the TVR auto-gear.

Real Photographs Co.

'Metro' class 2-4-0T No. 3586 on a Llantrisant to Pontypridd auto working, near Church Village, on 7th May, 1948.   *I.L. Wright*

TVR auto-trailer at Cowbridge just prior to World War I, having worked through from Pontypridd, passing over the Llantrisant branch *en route*.   *Welsh Industrial and Maritime Museum*

branches in the early 1890s; No. 54 failed at Taff Llantwit Colliery sidings on 6th August, 1894. By 1897 all workings from Cowbridge shed were covered by mixed traffic 0-6-2Ts. The 'M' class engines were joined by those of 'O' and 'O1' classes after 1894 and later by 'N' and 'O2' classes, all basically similar 0-6-2Ts. The working timetable for April 1897 gives a single Cowbridge-based goods working in the morning to Coke Ovens, returning via the Mwyndy branch, to Aberthaw. There were two Coke Ovens goods workings, one in the morning to Cowbridge and back and an afternoon return trip as far as Llantrisant. A morning Cardiff-based train worked over Llantrisant No. 1 Railway to Glyn Colliery, returning via Llantrisant Junction and the TVR main line, while an afternoon working reversed the procedure.

By 1903 the pattern of working had altered in favour of Cowbridge Shed, with two trips to Coke Ovens yard and back, one first thing in the morning and the other at midday. The first up train was assisted over the Llantrisant branch by a Coke Ovens engine which had worked out light to meet it at Llantrisant. Apart from this, only one goods working was operated by a Coke Ovens engine, but this had an interesting itinerary, working first to Glyn Colliery, then to Broviskin at the end of the Mwyndy branch, before returning to Coke Ovens. Another interesting working was that undertaken in the evening by a Merthyr engine to Llantrisant Common Junction and back. A single Cardiff working operated over Llantrisant No. 1 Railway *en route* to Glyn Colliery and back.

Passenger trains were usually hauled by Cowbridge engines, although in 1903 one such working was in the hands of a Coke Ovens engine. Trains usually consisted of seven coaches, with 4-wheeled stock of the 1870s and 80s used well into the present century. Six-wheeled stock, built in the 1890s, began to appear in the early 1900s. One of the main aims behind the introduction of steam railcars, or 'motor cars', on services such as those of the Llantrisant branch (from 1st May, 1905) was the reduction of costs on rural branch lines. Car No. 1 had been built by the TVR in 1903, very much as an experiment, and the last 'locomotive' to be constructed at the Company's West Yard works in Cardiff. The first 'production' cars (Nos. 2-7) were built by the Avonside Engine Co. of Bristol (engine units), and Bristol Wagon & Carriage Co. (coach units), and were introduced in 1904. A further batch of cars (Nos. 8-13) came from Kerr, Stuart and Co. (engine units) and Bristol W&C Co. (coach units) in 1905. This build was for third class only, but as the engine and coach units could be, and were, freely interchanged, engine units of this type were regularly seen on the Llantrisant branch, coupled with the earlier coach units.

In 1906 five more locomotive units (Nos. 14-18) built by Manning, Wardle & Co. of Leeds, with three coach units from Brush Electrical Engineering Co. of Loughborough, were introduced. These were of a larger more powerful type and were better suited to the Llantrisant branch with its severe gradients. Having said that, the cars as a whole were not entirely appropriate for the branch with its lengthy and difficult run and marked fluctuations in traffic. They were also prone to failure, usually from hot axle boxes, and their limited accommodation often led to complaints of overcrowding. To alleviate this last problem the TVR introduced trailers for the motor cars, but these were not permitted between Pontypridd and Llantrisant because of the severe gradients.

The Pontypridd train at Llantrisant on 20th May, 1950, with ex-TVR coaches Nos. W4025 and W1317 (converted from former motor cars Nos. 16 and 13). *I.L.Wright*

Ex-TVR Motor Car No. 13 (built Bristol Wagon & Carriage Co. in 1905) as coach No. W1317 at Pontypridd on 11th September, 1951. This was used on an evening working to Llantrisant, together with No. W4025. *H.C. Casserley*

Coach No. W4025 (originally TVR Motor Car No. 16, built Brush Electrical 1906) at Pontypridd on 11th September 1951, coupled to coach No. W1317. *H.C. Casserley*

Ex-GWR auto-trailer No. 108 stands in the sidings at Llantrisant on 5th May, 1951.
H.C. Casserley

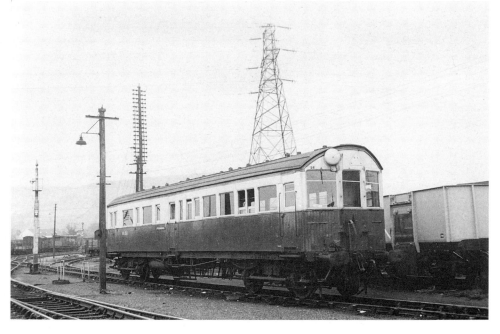

A peaceful interlude as branch line connections await the arrival of the main line train at Llantrisant in 1949. A '14XX' class 0-4-2T No. 1471 waits in the Penygraig bay with a Pontypridd auto-train, whilst 'Metro' class 2-4-0T and auto-trailer wait in the Cowbridge bay.   *L&GRP*

A loaded coke train, double-headed by two '56XX' class 0-6-2T engines, waits to depart from Cwm Colliery Siding ground frame for Treforest.   *R. Mason*

Towards the end of 1907 the three 'I' class 4-4-0Ts, built in 1884 and 1885, were fitted for auto-working and coupled with auto-trailers supplied by the Bristol W&C Co. One set, comprising an engine between a driving trailer composite and a driving trailer third, went to Cowbridge and worked over the Llantrisant branch, in place of one of the motor cars. In May 1908 the surviving locomotive and coaches working was withdrawn, any tail traffic over the Llantrisant branch being handled by the auto-train. The remaining motor car was usually one of the larger units of 1906. Between 1910 and 1912 six of the 'M1' class 0-6-2Ts were modified for auto-working. In December 1910 two bogie thirds were similarly converted and in 1912 two more auto-trailers were built by the Gloucester Railway Carriage & Wagon Co. With a total of four auto-sets available, the motor car was taken off the Llantrisant branch service. In 1913 the 'I' class 4-4-0T engines were replaced by auto-fitted 'M1' class 0-6-2Ts. From October 1917, as a wartime economy measure, only one auto-set was based at Cowbridge, with the other set being provided by Coke Ovens. As a result of this change, 'C' class 4-4-2Ts built in 1888 and 1891 and auto-fitted from 1916, made their appearance on the Llantrisant branch.

The working timetable for July 1914 shows a complicated pattern of goods and mineral train working over the Llantrisant branches. There were three Cowbridge workings to Coke Ovens and two Abercynon workings over the Llantrisant branch. The first Abercynon working terminated at Maesaraul Junction from where the engine banked the first up Cowbridge goods train back to Llantrisant Junction, returning from there to Llanharry Iron Ore Mine for iron ore and other traffic to Quakers Yard Junction, while the second worked from Abercynon to Broviskin and back. A Coke Ovens engine worked a local goods over the Treferig branch and to Llantrisant Common Junction, the train terminating at Llantwit or Common Branch Junction if there was no traffic beyond these places. On the Llantrisant No. 1 Railway a conditional mineral train ran from Waterhall Junction to Ely Tin Works, near Llantrisant station, from where it returned, via Llantwit, to Llantrisant Junction.

With the restoration of the passenger train service to its pre-war level in 1920, two sets were again based at Cowbridge. Auto-working was abandoned, with mixed traffic 'O' and 'O1' class 0-6-2Ts taking over all workings from that shed. These were joined, from July 1923, by ex TVR 'C' class 4-4-2Ts. After the closure of Cowbridge shed on 8th March, 1924, the passenger service was handled by Llantrisant engines, usually GWR '1076' class 0-6-0PTs, although some workings were provided by Coke Ovens shed.

Auto-working was re-introduced between Llantrisant and Pontypridd in 1931. At first, '517' class 0-4-2Ts shared the service with 'Metro' class 2-4-0Ts, but from 1937 the 'Metros' held sway. They were joined in 1936 by new Collett 0-4-2T No. 4871 (later 1471), which was to remain at Llantrisant until the withdrawal of the Llantrisant-Pengraig service in 1958. In the last years of the Llantrisant branch service, 'Metro' class No. 3586 was a regular performer, although other types appeared, including the auto-fitted '64XX' class 0-6-0PTs. One interesting working in later years was an early evening train from Pontypridd, consisting of an ex-TVR 'A' class 0-6-2T from Abercynon Shed hauling non-auto ex-TVR trailers Nos. 4025 and 1317, converted from steam motor-cars.

'57XX' class 0-6-0PT No. 3644 at Maesaraul Junction, with a gunpowder train from the ICI depot at the terminus of the Mwyndy branch. *R. Mason*

'56XX' class 0-6-2T No. 5694 takes water in the Cowbridge bay at Llantrisant on 5th August, 1958, whilst working a Treherbert to Porthcawl excursion. The engine had just run round its train, following its arrival from Pontypridd. *R. Darlaston*

Left: '94XX' class 0-6-0PT No. 8471 on a loaded Creigiau Quarry to Radyr limestone working, near Capel Llaniterne on Llantrisant No. 1 Railway. *I. Hatton-Evans*

Below: Change of engines at Cwm Colliery Sidings on 19th June, 1982, with No. 08 187, on loan from BR to the NCB, being replaced by No. 08 481
R.W. Ranson

Goods and mineral train working on the Llantrisant branches in the years following the Grouping established a pattern which was to last, in its basic form, until the end of steam and the line closures in 1964. Llantrisant engines handled up to three iron ore trains from Llanharry to Ffaldcaiach each day, but otherwise Llantrisant branch trains were in the hands of Coke Ovens or Abercynon engines. Early GWR 0-6-0Ts predominated at Llantrisant Shed, while ex-TVR 0-6-2Ts, altered to suit GWR tastes, were provided by the two former TVR sheds. These gradually gave way to more standard types, in particular the '57XX' 0-6-0PT and '56XX' 0-6-2T classes. Class '42XX' and '52XX' 2-8-0Ts were permitted to work the Llanharry-Ffaldcaiach iron ore trains over the Llantrisant branch provided the speed of the train did not exceed 20 mph at any point *en route*. With the cessation of this traffic in 1930, and the closure of Coke Ovens Engine Shed on 31st December, 1933, Abercynon engines came to predominate on goods and mineral train working on the Llantrisant branch. On the Llantrisant No. 1 Railway stone traffic from Creigiau Quarry was handled by Cardiff Canton engines, while coal from Cwm Colliery was worked by Radyr engines. Radyr engines later took over most workings on the No. 1 Railway.

The introduction of English Electric type '3' Co-Co diesels (later class '37') in August 1964 was accompanied by the complete reorganisation of train working on the Llantrisant branches. Traditional methods were swept away and complex new patterns of trip working devised, centred on Llantrisant, where a new diesel depot was established and the steam shed closed. The working timetable for April 1966 shows four diagrams for the Co-Cos, each including trips to Cwm Colliery or Creigiau Quarry, together with others to Clydach Vale and Coed Ely collieries on the Ely Valley branch and over the South Wales main line to such places as Severn Tunnel Junction, East Moors Steelworks and Margam Yard. In addition, a 350 hp diesel shunter (later class '08') was employed to shunt the yard at Llantrisant and to work the Mwyndy branch. In all, there were seven trips to Cwm and two to Creigiau, each day, at this time. By May 1982, the daily requirement at Llantrisant had come down to two class '37' and one class '08' locomotives, although there were still six trips to Cwm Colliery and back each day. For a time a class '08' shunter No. 08 487 was loaned to British Coal for work at Cwm Colliery, but this was returned to BR on 20th August, 1986.

After working the last coal train from Cwm Colliery on 2nd March, 1987, class '37' No. 37 244 remained at Llantrisant until 9th March, when it was transferred to Cardiff Canton. Llantrisant depot finally closed on Friday, 27th March, 1987.

Chapter Twelve

Finale or Encore?

The running of a last revenue train, in the form of an enthusiasts' excursion, on 11th April, 1987, appeared to mark the end of the story as far as the Cwm branch was concerned. The track remained in place, however, in view of the possibility that coal traffic might be restored *to* Cwm to serve the coke ovens, which continued in use after the closure of the colliery. In 1987 British Rail obtained Parliamentary powers to divert part of the Cwm branch near Cowbridge Road Crossing in connection with the building of Talbot Green Bypass. A temporary stop block was erected on the Llantrisant side of the level crossing in October 1989. The bypass was constructed on the route of the railway for a short distance and a new level crossing provided on the bypass itself, in place of Cowbridge Road Crossing, which was abolished. Talbot Green Bypass opened on 1st November, 1991, but it was not until March 1993 that track laying was completed on the new alignment of the Cwm branch, to the north of the bypass.

The decline of freight traffic on the railways of South Wales has been matched by a resurgence in the fortunes of local passenger services, helped by a very positive attitude towards new investment on the part of the local authorities. Following the successful re-opening of the Aberdare branch in October 1988, an ambitious scheme was developed to reinstate a passenger train service on the Maesteg branch in conjunction with the reintroduction of a local service between Bridgend and Cardiff. The Cardiff-Maesteg service was introduced on 28th September, 1992, with a new station at Pontyclun on the site of the former Llantrisant station. Such has been the success of this service, that it has been suggested that it should be augmented by a new Cardiff-Pontyclun and Beddau service, doubling the frequency between Cardiff and Pontyclun to half-hourly and running over the Cwm branch, with stations at Talbot Green, Llantrisant (Southgate), Beddau and Tynant. This chapter may not, therefore, be closed!

Bridge under the ex-TVR main line at Maesmawr, showing the course of a branch of the former Maesmawr Tramroad on the left.   *W. John*

133

Nature regains her own on the disused Cwm branch near Beddau in March 1995.   *W. John*

The goods shed at Cross Inn in a remarkably good state of preservation in March 1995. *W. John*

Appendix

Principal Acts of Parliament

Llantrissant and Taff Vale Junction Railway

24 & 25 Vict. Ch.li; 7th August, 1861
Incorporation of Company;
Three railways from TVR to EVR;
Purchase of Llantwit Vardre Railway;
Working and traffic agreements with TVR;
Provision of third rail and grant of running powers over EVR from Maesaraul Junction to south-east terminus of Mwyndy branch.

29 & 30 Vict. Ch.ccxlviii; 23rd July, 1866
Four railways from PHD&R to EVR.

33 & 34 Vict. Ch.lxxiii; 20th June, 1870
Extension of time for Railway No. 1 of 1866 Act;
Abandonment of Railway No. 2 of 1866 Act;
Confirmation of lease by TVR.

36 & 37 Vict. Ch.clv; 21st July, 1873
Extension of time for Railway No. 1 of 1866 Act;
Confirmation of agreement (25th March, 1873) between TVR and GWR and L&OR.

40 & 41 Vict. Ch.cxxxvii; 2nd August, 1877
Extension of time for Railway No. 1 of 1866 Act.

43 & 44 Vict. Ch.xxiv; 29th June, 1880
Extension of time for Railway No. 1 of 1866 Act.

Treferig Valley Railway

42 & 43 Vict. Ch.clxvi; 21st July, 1879
Incorporation of Company;
Three railways from Common Branch of L&TVJR;
Working and traffic agreements with TVR and GWR.

47 & 48 Vict. Ch.cxxix; 14th July, 1884
Additional capital;
Confirmation of lease by TVR.

Taff Vale Railway

52 & 53 Vict. Ch.cxciii; 26th August, 1889
Amalgamation of L&TVJR and Treferig Valley Railway with TVR.

Acknowledgements

I would like to thank all those who have helped in the preparation of this book. Special thanks must go to Tony Cooke, Graham Croad, John Dore-Dennis, Cliff Harris, John Hutton, Iorwerth Prothero, Dick Riley, Chris Taylor, and Ian Wright, and members of the Welsh Railways Research Circle, too numerous to mention. I would also like to thank my wife, Diana, for her support and interest throughout.

Bibliography

This book has been complied almost entirely from primary source material, including company minutes and various reports held at the Public Record Office, Kew, with use also being made of contemporary journals and newspapers. However, the following works have also been referred to.

E.L. Ahrons	*Locomotive and Train Working in the Latter Part of the 19th Century* (1923)
D.S. Barrie	*The Taff Vale Railway* (1962)
C. Chapman	*The Cowbridge Railway* (1984)
E.L. Chappell	*History of the Port of Cardiff* (1939)
J. Davies	*Cardiff and the Marquesses of Bute* (1981)
E.D. Lewis	*The Rhondda Valleys* (1958)
E.T. MacDermot	*History of the GWR* (1927)
J.H. Morris & L.J. Williams	*The South Wales Coal Industry 1841-1875* (1958)
E.R. Mountford	*GWR Absorbed Coaching Stock 1922/1923* (1978)
I.W. Prothero	*Barry Docks and Railways* (1994)
RCTS	*The Locomotives of the GWR Part 10* (1966)

A '56XX' class 0-6-2T and train silhouetted against the skyline at Common Branch Junction on 9th November, 1951. *Welsh Industrial and Maritime Museum*